— THE —
CLAIMS
GAME

The Tricks and Deceptive Tactics Insurance Companies Use to Underpay or Deny Your Claim

David Skipton, PCLA, LPCS, SPPA, AIC

ISBN: 978-1-4834-3701-9 (sc)
ISBN: 978-1-4834-3703-3 (hc)
ISBN: 978-1-4834-3702-6 (e)

Library of Congress Control Number: 2015913699

Lulu Publishing Services rev. date: 11/05/2015

I want to dedicate this work to my mentor, long-time business partner, and friend, Mr. Victor Dennis Beard, EGA (executive general adjuster), deceased. Victor was the most passionate, brilliant, and successful claims adjuster I have ever known. Victor gave me the highest standards by which to measure success and constantly challenged me to think through each coverage argument and claim situation to find the winning strategy for our clients. It was a joy to watch the "master" command the utmost respect from so many adversarial companies and their battalions of attorneys. They say that the greatest gift one can bestow upon another is the gift of knowledge; I thank you, Victor, for your generous gift, and I miss you.

David Skipton

CONTENTS

FOREWORD

Having read Mr. Skipton's book, "The Claims Game," I can recommend it to everyone who has a dispute with their insurer over damage to their home or business. Mr. Skipton provides insight into what causes some of the problems that occur and valuable advice on how to handle those problems when they do occur.

Review Provided by Former State Supreme Court Justice

(Name withheld by request)

*If you've suffered an insured loss to your business or home, **you need to read this book!***

My career as a public adjuster started with a personal experience on a multi-million dollar commercial claim that changed my life, as will the journey upon which you are about to embark. Whether your claim is large or small, the good news is that as an informed consumer of the insurance product you've purchased, the knowledge gained through this book will give you a great advantage in obtaining the fair settlement that you are owed. The bad news is that the adjuster assigned by the insurance company, handles claims like yours every day, and, while a personal experience for you, it is just everyday business for the adjuster and insurance company.

This book is full of actual examples encountered by Dave Skipton in the preparation of claims for their clients. I know they are true, accurate, and very common, as I have worked as a public adjuster for 30 years, and like Dave Skipton, I've experienced all these examples.

This year, I was selected by my peers as president of the National Association of Public Insurance Adjusters (NAPIA). Dave Skipton is one of my most trusted colleagues. He has written a hard hitting expose' and excellent resource to help consumers understand their options after a loss and guide them in making good choices as they pursue the fair claim settlement that they paid their hard earned premiums for.

R. Scott deLuise, CPPA, SPPA, CCIM

INTRODUCTION

This book is intended to provide consumers with an easy-to-understand overview of how the insurance-claims process works in today's profit-hungry world of insurance. Insurance companies have discovered a new source of revenue, and it comes directly from the pockets of their most vulnerable customers. This new revenue source is from claims payments, and if you have filed a claim, you are likely to be one of their unwitting victims.

If you have just recently had a loss, you should jump to the appendices at the back of this book and read them first. These appendices are designed to provide you with important information to use to protect yourself from predatory claims-handling practices.

The aftermath of a serious loss event and the uncertainty that it brings can be extremely unsettling. Few people will ever deal with a major property claim, and most are not well equipped to deal with the claims process. As such, most of them are forced to rely upon the guidance and goodwill of their insurance company to assist them in their recovery. Unfortunately, all too often, the guidance provided is not so much aimed at the customer's recovery as it is at minimizing the cost of the claim to the insurance company.

This book will not train you to adjust your own claim. It takes years of training and a much more extensive curriculum than is practical in one book. But, the improper claims practices described in this book will help you identify wrongdoing and alert you about what to look for to assure that you are being dealt with fairly by your insurance company. Knowing how the game is played can empower the consumer to take actions to protect his or her interests. Understanding the claims game can provide a measure of clarity in the uncertain world of those who have suffered a catastrophic loss. It can also be your first step to a proper and fair recovery.

The stories in this book are all true accounts of claims practices that we have encountered over the past decade. The names of those identified in this book have been changed to protect their privacy and we have purposely not identified the insurance companies, as condemning individual companies is beyond the scope of this book.

We have tried to make this book as interesting as possible, but let's be honest; insurance is not the most interesting subject, unless of course you have just experienced a major loss. Insurance claims can be highly complex, and, like fingerprints, each claim has its own unique characteristics.

This book should serve as a guide to help you navigate the claims process and more effectively work with your insurance company and certainly on more equal grounds.

CHAPTER 1

Not Your Daddy's Insurance Company

Bill and Ruth had just returned home to Sun City, Arizona, after spending a few weeks visiting friends and family in Kansas. As they pulled into the driveway, they noticed water pouring out from under the garage door and running down the driveway. After seventeen hours on the road, this was the last thing they needed.

Upon opening the garage door, their worst fears were confirmed, as their home was several inches deep in water. This was no ordinary water leak; this was from a high-pressure line, and it must have gone on for days, as the water damage stretched from one end of their beautiful home to the other. This was the Arizona retirement home that they had dreamed of for years, and it was nearly perfect, situated on a Sun City golf course in a gorgeous retirement community. Bill had taken pride in perfecting every detail to entertain guests, with an impressive outdoor bar that even included draft beer. He hadn't missed a thing in creating his dream home.

Bill grew up dirt poor, but through hard work and perseverance, he worked his way up the corporate ladder at Ford Motor Company, rising from doing odd jobs in the parts department to eventually becoming a vice president. Bill was truly a self-made man who prided himself on having the best, be it his perfectly maintained cars or the dozens of exotic designer shoes he had purchased. These things, as well as his home, were symbols of a life that was both hard earned and well deserved.

But Bill and Ruth's dream was now threatened by an unforeseen water-pipe break that wreaked destruction upon their home and all of their belongings. Bill's first reaction was to call his insurance agent, who politely gave him the name of an emergency-services company that specialized in water extractions. Then Bill remembered that an old friend from Ford had gone to work recently in the insurance-claims business, so his next call was to his friend to ask for advice on how to handle this situation.

Bill's friend had recently come to work in the marketing department of our firm in our Dallas, Texas, office. He explained to Bill how, for a small fee, we represent the policyholder's interests in settling insurance claims. Bill knew that his situation was well beyond his ability to handle on his own, and he knew from his years in the business world that leaving the insurance company to set the value of his claim on its own did not make sense. So after meeting with us, he retained our firm to represent him on his claim.

Even though Bill had purchased a very good policy from one of the largest insurance companies in America, it took the claims department fourteen days before representatives even made their first visit to Bill's home. During this first meeting, representatives from the insurance company spent several hours writing up their damage evaluation for Bill's home on their laptop computer.

At the end of this first meeting, they confirmed that they had completed their damage evaluation but told us that they were not authorized to share their evaluation until it was approved by management. It was another thirty-six days before we finally got a glimpse at their evaluation, and we were extremely disappointed to find that the total was for less than half of the damages we had agreed upon at their initial inspection.

We quickly proceeded to prepare a reconciliation to itemize the differences between their evaluation and ours, and we set another meeting to resolve those differences. At that meeting, the insurance company representatives politely advised us that they would take our concerns under consideration, discuss them with their management, and get back to us. It was all too clear that the adjusters representing one of the largest insurance companies in the country had no authority to settle a claim and instead had to ask for approval to pay the claim from supervisors who had never even seen the damages. It had now been three more weeks, and we still awaited their reply.

After more than two months of the insurer's unreasonable delays and gamesmanship, we were informed that Bill was experiencing high anxiety and significant stress, which was likely the result of his unresolved claim situation. In fact, Bill even went to see his doctor over these issues. People react to stressful situations in different ways, and medical science has shown that there is a causative link between emotional stress and physical manifestations.

Today, we learned that Bill was admitted last night to the hospital following a severe stroke and was in the intensive-care unit in serious condition. The doctors performed surgery early this morning, but whether Bill will make a full recovery is in question. You might think, *All this over an insurance claim?* But what you must remember is that this is a lot more than just an insurance claim to Bill; this is his life and his life's accumulation of things that are all personal and important to him and his wife. The water loss was only the first tragedy. The bigger tragedy ended up being the insurance company's game-playing and the excessive delays in the claims process that are deliberately designed to wear down the consumer and reduce the insurance companies' liability for damages.

At this point, it is unclear how Bill and Ruth's situation will turn out or how well Bill will recover from the stroke. But what is clear is that the actions of Bill's insurance company were not undertaken by accident. This is just one example of the insurance industry's high-stakes game of low-balling the customer for its own profit. This practice is far more common today than it was in years past. Insurance companies know that by offering low-ball claim settlements and then delaying the process for as long as possible, they can get many claimants to simply give up and just take what they can get without a fight.

Let's face it; most people who have experienced a loss do not want to deal with years of litigation in order to be paid fairly for their claim. They just want their lives put back together as quickly as possible. The insurance companies know this and use this motivation against their customers to reduce the companies' claims payments. You see, every dollar saved on claims payments is another dollar of profit that drops directly to the insurance company's bottom line.

To the insurance industry, this is nothing more than a *Claims Game*. To the homeowner or business owner who may have just lost everything he or she owns to a fire, windstorm, or some other tragedy, it certainly is no game. But the sad truth is that to the insurance company, the consumer has become a pawn in a high-stakes game of "catch us if you can" and "hide and go seek" your claim payments. We have experienced these real-life circumstances with our clients for more than two decades, which gave rise to the idea for this book.

The problems with achieving fair claim settlements have become epidemic in America, as insurance companies have become more blatant than ever before in their disrespect for their customers and more indifferent to fulfilling their contractual agreements. And justice is not easily found, as some recent court rulings have gutted consumers' ability to hold insurance companies accountable for their wrongful conduct through bad-faith punitive-damage awards.

To help you better understand the rules that govern insurance, let's briefly explain the term *tort* and the concept of insurance "bad faith." A tort is a wrongful act, other than a breach of contract that unfairly causes someone else to suffer loss or harm. The remedy for a tort in civil courts is a monetary award for the damages suffered. In Arizona, as in most other jurisdictions, the tort of bad faith arises when an insurer intentionally denies or fails to process or pay a claim without a reasonable basis for doing so. These courts recognize that an insurance policy (contract) is not an ordinary commercial bargain and that implicit in an insurance contract and in the insurance relationship is the insurer's promise to play fairly with its insured.

The Arizona courts described this duty in the *Rawlings* case, in which the Arizona Supreme Court concluded that the insurer has "some duties of a fiduciary nature," including "equal consideration, fairness and honesty."[1] The insurance company has an obligation to immediately conduct a reasonable investigation, act reasonably in evaluating the claim, and act promptly in

---

[1]   Rawlings v. Apodaca, 151 Ariz. 149; 726 P.2d 565 (1986)

paying a legitimate claim. If an insurer acts unreasonably in the manner in which it processes a claim, it can be held liable for bad faith, which can result in punitive damages.

Bad faith and punitive damages are concepts that were designed into our legal system to deter businesses and individuals from deliberately engaging in wrongful conduct. The idea is to award punitive damages to the wronged party to discourage a specific wrongdoer and other potential future wrongdoers from knowingly and deliberately engaging in wrongful conduct in the future. An award of punitive damages is intended to place a monetary penalty on the wrongdoer to deter misconduct and make such misconduct too expensive to be a viable business practice. It's sort of a legal version of "hit them where it hurts most—in their wallets." For instance, if an insurance company deliberately engages in wrongful conduct, as described above, and is later held liable to pay only the contract damages that it owed in the first place, where is the incentive for it to act properly?

One major factor that has set in motion the increase we are seeing in wrongful claims conduct was the United States Supreme Court's ruling in *Campbell v. State Farm,*[2] wherein the court ruled that a $145 million punitive-damages award that was upheld against State Farm by the Utah Supreme Court was excessive. The United States Supreme Court held that even in the most extreme circumstances, the multiplier for punitive-damage awards should not exceed a "single-digit" multiplier of the contract damages. What this means is that a multiplier of nine times the actual damages is as much as the Supreme Court believes is reasonable under the law. The court's decision was based on the "due process" clause found in the Fourteenth Amendment of the Constitution.

Many state courts have taken this decision and narrowed the punitive-damage award guidelines even further; some have ruled that punitive damages should not exceed a ratio of one to one. What this means to a consumer is that the courts have essentially given the insurance companies a license to steal from their customers. How do you deter a multibillion-dollar insurance company from committing egregious acts against its

---

[2]   Campbell v. State Farm, 538 U.S. 408; 123 S. Ct. 1513; 155 L. Ed. 2d 585; (2003)

policyholders if the mechanism of justice has no teeth? In particular, if an insurance company cheats millions of people out of small to moderate amounts of money, this is highly profitable for the insurance company but very hard for the cheated consumer to make right.

The best defense consumers had before *Campbell* was that a deliberately deceptive insurance practice, even over a relatively small amount of money, could result in a huge punitive-damage award. This concept is best illustrated by the Arizona court's ruling in *Hawkins v. Allstate*[3], where Allstate was caught wrongfully withholding thirty-five dollars per claim for cleaning of the vehicles on total loss auto claims. The court looked at the vast number of claims Allstate had processed in this manner over a certain period of time in order to determine the reasonable punishment. This pre-*Campbell* ruling ultimately cost Allstate $3.5 million in punitive damages. That's right, $3.5 million on a damage claim of thirty-five dollars. What better way to get an incredibly rich insurance company's attention than to expose them to substantial punitive damages for willful breaches of their duty to act in good faith?

Today, under *Campbell*, the most *Hawkins* would be able to recover would be $315 in punitive damages, or nine times the contract damages amount. For a multi-billion-dollar insurance company, this potential penalty limitation is certainly not much of a deterrent. So the reality is that insurance companies have been emboldened and have become more difficult than ever to hold accountable for their wrongful conduct. And this lack of consequences has exacerbated the problems consumers face when they file an insurance claim.

Even more disturbing is that the smaller the amount of the dispute, the more unlikely it is that the customer will receive justice. For instance, let's assume that your claim was significant—say, $100,000—but through a painstaking process of battling with your insurer, you have gotten the difference down to $20,000. What attorney is going to take on an insurance bad-faith case for $20,000? While you may get lucky and find one, the chances are he will not be a top-tier attorney, because there is simply not

---

[3]   Hawkins v. Allstate, 152 Ariz. 490; 733 P.2d 1073; (1987)

enough potential recovery to make this fight worth the attorney's time. And a battle it will be, as insurance companies fight consumers even harder in litigation than they do during the claims process. Insurance companies fully realize they are unlikely to be held accountable for wrongdoing on these smaller claims, which essentially gives them a license to steal.

It is a travesty that consumers must hire claims professionals or attorneys to get what they paid for when they bought their insurance policies. Even more outrageous is the fact that consumers must fight and even litigate to hold their insurance companies accountable and to assure that they are paid fairly and in accordance with the policy's promise of coverage. Much has been written on this subject, including a very insightful investigative report several years ago in *Bloomberg Magazine* called "The Insurance Hoax."[4] This Bloomberg article exposed the unreasonable tactics used by the nation's largest insurance company to underpay homeowner's claims in southern California following the 2003 wildfires, while the insurer was raking in record-breaking profits. Unfortunately, things have only gotten worse since that article was written. This is the new reality of the insurance business today. It is important for consumers to be aware—not only of the game, but of how it is played, as knowing and understanding the game can place the consumer on more equal footing with the insurance company and the adjuster.

---

[4]   David Dietz and Darrell Preston *Bloomberg Markets Magazine* September 2007

CHAPTER TWO

"Trouble ... Trouble, Trouble:"
A New Perspective

What we often hear from potential clients is, "Why would I need my own adjuster? Doesn't the insurance company provide me with an adjuster?" The answer to this question is both yes and no. Yes, they do provide an adjuster to investigate and settle your claim; but no, that adjuster does not represent your interests. Instead, that adjuster is there to represent the insurance company's interests.

The business of insurance has undergone significant changes in America throughout the last twenty years. Gone are the days when an insurance company viewed its job as a true fiduciary responsibility of collecting premiums from a large group of people and paying out fairly to customers who experience a loss, thus fulfilling the promise to protect its customers in their time of need. Have you noticed how all the old commercials and slogans that used to run constantly on television and radio have all changed in their messaging? Gone are all the timeless slogans telling you how much you can depend upon your insurance company to protect you in the event of a loss and what great partners in the community they are—slogans like: "You're in Good Hands;" "Like a Good Neighbor;" and, of course, "Fast, Fair, and Friendly."

Today, insurance companies' commercials are designed to send a completely different message. It seems that they intentionally downplay how much of a partner they will be during a time of loss and instead have adopted more generic themes, such as that losses can happen and you need to insure yourself from them. This is apparent in ads like Allstate's "Mayhem" commercials, where Mayhem is causing all sorts of destruction, and Liberty Mutual's "Humans: imperfect people living in an imperfect world. Responsibility; what's your policy?"

According to Consumer Reports[5] ratings, Allstate and Liberty Mutual are both near the bottom of their list of good insurance companies. It has been our experience that you may not truly understand what mayhem is until you file a claim with Allstate. And from our dealings with Liberty Mutual, it is clear that if responsibility was actually was their policy, we'd be out of a job.

There are also those cute new "Farmer's University" commercials, but it is still unclear as to how the stupid looks on those student adjusters' faces might inspire people to want them adjusting their next insurance claim. And, of course, our favorite because we are dog lovers: the Traveler's dog with the bone and the music playing the words, "Trouble ... trouble, trouble" in the background as he dreams about losing his bone. The poor dog doesn't realize that, based on our experience, the insurance company he insured his bone with is the one most likely to actually steal it!

The changes in the way insurance companies market their products were not made by accident. They are a clear indication of how they have changed their relationship with their customers. They no longer care if you are unhappy with their claims settlements or that you might decide to change insurance companies. There are millions of other customers out there that are equally unhappy with their current insurance companies who will be knocking on their doors for a new insurance policy. The business of insurance is no longer about providing a good product, good service, and customer retention; it is purely and simply about reducing claims costs and increasing net profits.

We constantly talk with people who are under the delusion that their insurance company actually values their business. We often hear comments

---

[5]   *Consumer Reports* May 2014

of shock, like this one from a recent client: "I have been a customer of XYZ Insurance for twenty-eight years and I have never had a claim until now—and then they just drop me over this one claim!" Most people find it hard to believe how quickly they can go from being a valued customer (a loss-free, premium-paying policyholder) to a liability (a customer with a claim to be paid).

The modern view of insurance companies is about profits, profits, profits—and more profits. This is what drives their management and the enormous bonuses they receive, and it is what satisfies their shareholders. How did this transformation happen? How did we get here?

Many industry experts agree that these changes have a direct correlation with the separation of Allstate Insurance Company from its parent company, Sears, Roebuck & Company, in the early 1990s. [6] For those of you not from that generation, up until the early 1990s, Allstate was a part of Sears. In the 60s and 70s, we could go down to the local Sears & Roebuck store with Dad to buy a new hammer, pick up a couple dress shirts for Dad, and pay our car insurance bill to the handy agent, who, for years, usually sat at an Allstate booth near the escalator.

Around 1992, the Allstate Insurance Company engaged the services of international business-consulting firm McKinsey & Company, with the idea of remaking the company from the top down to make it more profitable. You may recall that McKinsey was associated with the collapsed Enron Corporation, which was called "The house that McKinsey built."[7]

For more than a year, McKinsey's legions of MBAs worked in every department analyzing Allstate's business operations. They looked analytically at every process as a function that could either generate more revenues or as an expense that could be better managed. McKinsey made its recommendations to Allstate via several PowerPoint slide presentations in 1992, but it wasn't until 2001 that the contents of these presentations became public, and only via a direct court order and after a monumental effort by Allstate's attorneys to keep their contents secret. [8]

---

[6]   *Bloomberg Report* September 2007

[7]   www.theguardian.com/business/2002/mar/24/enron.theobserver

[8]   www.propertycasualty360.com/2008/04/07/allstate-releases-entire-mckinsey-report-for-review

What McKinsey recommended was a complete transformation of the "philosophy" of Allstate's business model from the traditional customer-service focus to a profit-centric focus. McKinsey easily identified that the largest expense on the insurance company's profit and loss statement was for claims expenses (i.e., claims payments). So the natural solution to increasing Allstate's profits was, quite simply: reduce claims payments.

In order to better understand this monumental transformation of the business of insurance, it is important that you understand some of the basic tenets of insurance. The first is the indemnity principle, which is the overall purpose of property insurance. These policies promise to indemnify the policyholders, or restore them to the same financial position after the loss as they were before the loss. To indemnify someone is to make him or her whole. So under a fire-insurance policy, in the event of a fire, the insurance company promises to make the policyholder whole, up to the limits of the policy, in exchange for the policyholder's payment in the form of a premium.

Another important concept is that of the fiduciary principle, which has been the basic tenant of insurance law for nearly a century. The fiduciary principle was designed to balance the relationship between the insurance company and the policyholder. Under this principle, the insurance companies act much like a bank, holding the insured's money (premiums) and, of course, investing it until these funds are needed to pay out on a claim. It is a sacred trust placed with these insurance companies; thereby, they hold all of these policyholders' premiums in an account and then pay out fairly to restore those insureds that have suffered a covered loss.

The changes recommended by McKinsey & Company and then implemented by Allstate completely transformed the business of insurance, and not just for Allstate; they would ultimately change the entire insurance industry. The changes implemented transformed the insurance industry from the traditional business model of collecting premiums from a large group of customers and then paying the fair value for claims to those who incur a loss (a fiduciary responsibility) to a profit-focused model that ignored the fair indemnification of the policyholder to restore him to his pre-loss financial condition. Likewise, it simultaneously ignored other business principles, like customer satisfaction and customer retention, in favor of profits. Under this new philosophy, the expense of claims payments was now fair game to manage "for profit," and the cost of claims was now viewed as a profit center to pad their bottom line.

To better understand the changes that were being recommended, we need look no further than some of McKinsey's PowerPoint slides that were used in the presentation to the executives of Allstate. The most telling of these slides suggested that the business of insurance is a "Zero Sum Game."[9] This means that in order for someone to win, someone must lose. To put this idea into better perspective, let's rephrase this as it was to be applied at Allstate: "If Allstate is to win, its customers must lose."[10] It is an interesting business philosophy. How many policies do you think they would sell using this as their advertising slogan? Imagine if they changed their slogan from "You're in good hands with Allstate" to "If Allstate is going to make a huge profit, our customers must lose."

It seems that McKinsey's team of MBAs must have taken the lessons from the 1987 movie *Wall Street* to heart. You may recall Gordon Gekko's (Michael Douglas's character's) infamous line, "Greed is good!" This was the revolutionary new business philosophy that was being proposed to Allstate.

Other slides suggested that Allstate offer a quick, low-ball claim settlement, and if the customer did not take it, then it was time to "Put down the Good Hands and Pick up the Boxing Gloves."[11] Another slide focused on other opportunities for Allstate to improve profits by working to keep their policyholders from retaining professional representation, stating, "Even greater opportunity exists to prevent claimants from becoming represented (Payments on represented claims is on average five times the size of unrepresented claims.)"[12] In other words, keep our policyholders from hiring representation because it will cost us more money.

---

[9]   Victoria Pynchon Negotiation Law Blog "The Zero Sum Game Allstate's McKinsey Documents"

[10]   Victoria Pynchon Negotiation Law Blog "The Zero Sum Game Allstate's McKinsey Documents"

[11]   From the McKinsey/Allstate Documents

[12]   From the McKinsey/Allstate Documents

And, of course, the most famous of their slides gave this new philosophy for doing business a moniker. They called it the "Three Ds," which stood for *delay, deny,* and *defend.* In other words, *delay* the claim as long as possible, *deny* claims as often as they can, and then *defend* these denials to the end. Make the process so difficult that consumers just give up rather than fight.

In his book *From Good Hands to Boxing Gloves: The Dark Side of Insurance,*[13] attorney and author David Berardinelli brilliantly illustrates to the reader how the changes implemented by Allstate fly in the face of proper insurance conduct. He compares buying of a can of peas to buying an insurance policy. In his example, he suggests: What if you go to the store and buy a ten-ounce can of peas, but when you get home and open the can, you find it only contains seven ounces of peas? You take the can of peas back to the store and complain, and they give you another can of peas. However, when you get home and open the can, you find that it, too, has only seven ounces of peas in it. Of course, your first thought would be that this must be some kind of mistake. Maybe the machine needs to be recalibrated. But, what if you found out that the pea company had deliberately set its machine to only fill the ten-ounce can with seven ounces of peas so as to produce windfall profits for the pea company's shareholders and huge bonuses for its executives? Most people would call this fraud.

Allstate Insurance Company's implementation of this new claims-handling philosophy had dramatic effects on the company's operating income. In the ten-year period before implementation of the McKinsey program, Allstate's average annual pre-tax operating income was approximately $82 million per year. In the eleven-year period after implementation of the McKinsey program, Allstate's average pre-tax operating income grew to $2.5 billion annually, an incredible 3,335 percent increase. It did not take long for other insurance companies and their stockholders to take notice and begin the implementation of similar changes to duplicate these sorts of profit results for themselves and their shareholders. And McKinsey was not the only one making these types of bold recommendations. About this same

---

[13] David Berardinelli Good Hands To Boxing Gloves,

time, another major consulting firm, Accenture, was giving similar advice to its insurance company clients.[14]

This new focus on claims expenses as a profit center has completely changed the relationship between the insurance company and the consumer. Now, getting fair treatment on the settlement of claims is unlikely to be achieved without the services of a claims professional, such as a public adjuster or an attorney.

People are, by nature, resistant to change, and insurance-company employees are no exception. To curb internal resistance from the claims departments, the insurance companies have, little by little, pushed out those seasoned company adjusters who resisted these new claim procedures. Many of these seasoned adjusters knew that they were being asked to handle claims in a manner that was contrary to the practices and procedures that they had learned through their years of insurance training. Those who were willing to stay were forced to accept the new claims-handling procedures or else they were replaced with new, inexperienced, and poorly or intentionally mistrained adjusters. The old industry adage is that the more educated the adjuster, the more he will pay on claims. The reason for this is that a competent professional knows what truly should be paid under the policy.

In our interactions with many of these older and more seasoned professional adjusters, it was made quite clear that they were not happy with the way their claims-handling practices were being changed. Most were reluctant to process claims in the manner in which they are now expected to, so many of them have either retired or they may have sucked up their pride, turned a blind eye to these practices, and are simply counting the days until retirement.

Then, of course, there are those that stayed who have bought into the new claims philosophy. This group of adjusters is the worst of the worst, as they are active participants in the abusive tactics being employed in the settlement of claims. These "company men" are willing to do whatever it takes to gain favor with management.

---

[14] www.accenture.com/us-en/Pages/service-insurance-claims-components...

The newly hired adjusters do not know any better than what they have been taught by the company on claims handling in their two-week training programs. There is no way in the time currently being allotted to properly train an adjuster to investigate claims, determine coverage, and estimate the value of loss. They rely upon their managers, who tell customers that "our policy does not cover this or that." They are being deliberately sent out to settle claims with little knowledge or, even worse, misinformation.

We often have encounters with adjusters who spew the company line and tell us, "Our policy does not owe to match." Yet, when we hand them a copy of the policy and tell them to point out the language in the policy that says the company does not owe to match, they routinely refuse to even look at the policy. Most often, they tell us that it is in the policy and they are not obligated to show us where this provision is.

These "new age" claims adjusters are being assisted by insurance restoration contractors who routinely assist in preparing significantly deficient loss evaluations to gain favor with the insurance company. They are also being directed by management to work with approved experts/ consultants who routinely report that there is no damage or that the damage is from another cause of loss not covered in the policy.

This new breed adjuster handles claims under a different playbook than in the past. Gone are the days when an adjuster had reasonable settlement authority to resolve claims up to his authority limit. In the old days, as adjusters became more experienced in claims handling, their settlement authority was increased by management, giving them the ability to use their superior training and skills to settle claims fairly and in accordance with the terms of the policy.

Today, few insurers give adequate settlement authority to their adjusters, and many now give virtually no authority at all. We are constantly engaged with senior large-loss adjusters who have very little in settlement authority and must go through this same process of approval to get claim payments issued.

Most insurers have gone to a claim-manager or claim-committee review system, where the field adjuster has no authority whatsoever to issue claim payments. Today's adjuster prepares his report and makes his recommendation for settlement of the claim to a claims manager or claims committee, who review his report and either approve it or requests revisions. We assume that when they request a revision, it is not to pay the customer more money. And how are claims managers or committee members in a better position to determine the fair value of a claim that they have never seen?

This process makes the job of settling a claim far more time-consuming and difficult because we typically wait weeks for a management response, and all claim negotiations must be communicated through the adjuster, who is just a message boy in this process. Not only must you convince the adjuster of the proper payment of damages; you must also train him how to convince his manager or claim committee of their necessity.

To give you a clearer understanding of how these changes can lead to excessive delays in claim payments, the following quotation is from an e-mail we recently received regarding a claim that has been in processing by one of the three largest insurers in the nation for more than a year and a half:

> "My timeline from last week was delayed as the payment has been sent up from my supervisor, to the manager, to the territory manager, then to the regional manager. They have a meeting to approve tomorrow, as I have been routinely asking for status checks on the approval."

The process for approving claim payments has been deliberately modified to cause an intentional delay in the payment of claims. Instead of having a competent adjuster who has authority to issue claim payments, the adjusters today must go to their supervisor, to a manager, to a territory manager, and then to a regional manager before a payment can be issued for $30,000.

We believe that handling claims in this manner is a violation of the promise of the policy, which says the insurance company will negotiate the claim with you, the consumer, or with your representative. If you or your representative never get an audience (meeting) with someone from the insurance company who actually has authority to negotiate the settlement of your claim, how does this claims system fulfill the company's promise? Most policies contain language that generally states: "We (the insurance company) will adjust the loss with You (the insured)," but how can they fulfill this promise, if you never get to see the man behind the curtain or actually engage in negotiations with him?

Throughout the last ten years, these new procedures for claims handling seem to have gone on steroids, as we are seeing an ever-increasing trend of wrongful denials of coverage; significant underpayment of claims (low-balling); deliberate omissions of damages; and an array of other improper claims-handling practices. This new process has also spawned a drastic increase in the numbers of insurance experts/consultants, who are more than happy to do the insurance industry's bidding for them. Insurance companies are now constantly in need of expert reports that say there is no damage to the insured's property or that say the damages are related to something other than that which is covered by the insurance policy.

It is estimated that fewer than 5 percent of all claimants retain professional representation to settle their claims. If you are one of the many who are trying to deal with the aftermath of a major property-damage claim, it is our hope and purpose in this book to arm you with information that will help you to identify some of the tricks and deceptions that are most commonly used by the insurance companies today to intentionally underpay your claim.

CHAPTER THREE

Rules of the Game

In order to compete in the insurance industry's high-stakes "Claims Game," you must first understand the game and how it is played by the insurance companies. As in the game of chess, you cannot win if you do not know how the pieces move. In the Claims Game, the moves are not just about strategy; they start with understanding what everyone's interest is in your claims proceeds. Once you understand all the varied interests, you can begin to make good decisions to protect your own interests, instead of relying upon other people to tell you what to do. This will help you to develop a winning strategy.

The insurance company's first move is most often to send out a very charming claims adjuster to set your mind at ease that they are there to help you through this tragic event. He often comes with a checkbook in hand, ready to write you a relatively insignificant check to help you through the next few days. He will oftentimes warn you about all the "predatory public adjusters" who will try to sign you to a contract. This warning is often echoed by insurance agents and many of the insurance industry's restoration contractors. They will explain that public adjusters cannot get you any more than the insurance company is going to pay you anyway without their help, so by engaging them, you are just giving way some of your money. So, as a public service and out of the goodness of their hearts, they will tell you to avoid these public adjuster people. Are you overwhelmed by their concern yet?

The reality is often far different. As in any industry, there are both good and bad representatives, and public adjusting is no exception. Whether or not you decide to retain a public adjuster should be your decision alone, and it should not be made without careful consideration. The larger point here is that it is not your money that the insurance company is truly concerned with. They are concerned that, as you will recall from the previous chapter, "represented claims payout five times more than unrepresented claims." So the insurance company has a serious financial interest in discouraging claimants from hiring representation. Remember that in the insurance company's profit and loss statement, claim payments is the largest expense item. For every dollar saved in claims payments, that dollar flows through the financial report to the bottom line; i.e., the net profit.

Next, you might question why your agent, whom you have known for years, might care if you retain representation. After all, he is supposed to be on your side in this matter. The truth is that many agents have their own incentive to keep you from hiring representation. Most agents are paid based upon a formula that takes the total of the premiums collected on the insurance policies they sell and then subtracts the amount of claims paid out on those policies, before they calculate their sales commissions and/or annual bonus.

A few years ago, in a litigated claim, we had an agent who was questioned under oath as to why the insurance company's claim file showed that he had called both the adjuster and the claims manager multiple times to object to their intended payment of this huge fire-loss claim. He refused to accept the adjuster's determination that the claim was legitimate and went over his head to his supervisor and eventually was successful in getting the insurance company to deny coverage for the loss. After hours of excruciating questioning, he finally admitted that when the company was eventually forced by the evidence to pay this claim, it wiped out his substantial five-figure year-end bonus.

So your agent may or may not really be concerned with your interests as much as his own. This is certainly not an indictment of all agents. Most are good people who are truly interested in seeing their customers receive fair treatment. However, unfortunately, human nature cannot be blindly dismissed. There are some who will place their own financial interests above their customers' interests. Which agent you have is something you will need to decide for yourself. Our purpose here is to simply explain the varying interests when a claim is filed.

Why would a restoration contractor care if you hire a public adjuster? Most restoration contractors get the majority of their business from insurance companies, and many public adjusters have their own preferred contractors. Insurance restoration contractors rely heavily upon insurance companies to make their living. So if they can encourage consumers to not hire a public adjuster, they stand a much better chance of getting the job themselves, and, at the very least, they are earning brownie points with the assigned adjuster, who will likely respond favorably with other work for them.

More importantly, if you do retain the insurance company's preferred contractor, there is a reasonable chance that this contractor is more interested in the insurance company's interests than in yours as their customer. Just as with agents and public adjusters, the restoration contractor likewise has a financial incentive to favor the insurance company, as they get much of their work from them. If a dispute arises over whether or not the interior walls can be saved, whose side do you think the contractor is really on? Hopefully, he is on yours.

Another financial interest in your insurance-claim proceeds is that of the adjuster who is assigned to settle your claim. While it is considered improper within the insurance industry for an insurance company to provide financial incentives to their adjusters, which might encourage them to underpay claims, the fact is that adjuster bonuses are still commonplace, and they can significantly impact your claim settlement.

Having been involved in many dozens of insurance bad-faith litigations, we find that most insurance companies have some sort of performance-bonus program to incentivize their adjusters to meet the company's objectives. Over the years, this practice has been the source of many lawsuits, where the courts have ruled this practice to be a violation of the insurance company's duty of good faith under the insurance policy. Due to these costly bad-faith rulings, these programs have become more discreet in their true purpose by including other metrics such as good customer service, good claims-handling practices, how quickly the claim is closed, and other measures of their performance.

But make no mistake about it, nearly all of these programs contain some element that is tied to the financial performance of the insurance company and, in reality, we believe that this is actually their true measure of performance. While we have had most adjusters emphatically deny, even under oath, that they get any incentives for the company's financial performance, once we question them further and get into the details of their bonus programs, it is clear that most have hidden incentives built into their bonus programs.

Insurance companies are constantly focused on controlling costs. Adjusters can save very little money on office supplies, but significant underpayments of claims can drastically improve the insurance company's bottom line.

In the insurance business, the most important measure of profitability is known as the combined ratio, which is the claims expenses, plus the other cost of claims, divided by the total premiums collected. This ratio helps insurance companies to measure their performance. Nearly every adjuster bonus program we have seen, no matter how well it is disguised, includes the metric of meeting the company's combined ratio objectives. You might wonder how this is important to you.

When you have a claim, the cost of your claim to the insurance company gets added into the combined ratio along with all the other claims and claim expenses. The less money the adjuster pays you, the better the company's combined ratio becomes. If claim adjusters are incentivized to reduce claim payments to secure substantial bonuses, this creates a significant conflict of interest, and it can affect their ability to be objective in their loss determinations.

In the insurance litigation business, we refer to these types of adjuster incentive programs as "institutional bad faith" programs. It is considered bad faith for an insurance company to create a program that encourages their adjusters or provides an incentive for them to underpay a legitimate claim. Most insurance companies have taken drastic steps to hide or mask these programs in response to large bad-faith damages awards, but the fact is, most still have some bonus program that considers the company's meeting of their combined-ratio or financial goals.

Another interest in your claim proceeds is that of the emergency-services restoration company. These are the people that your agent or the person at the insurance company's claims hotline refer you to immediately to assist in the cleanup and security of the property until they get an adjuster assigned to your claim. This is the first step in the claims process to put you on the road to recovery. These alleged "experts" will come into your home or business to give you advice on what must be done to protect the property from further damage. This advice is important because under the policy's terms and conditions is the requirement that you (the insured) take all reasonable steps to protect the property from further damage.

These emergency-restoration contractors come referred by your insurance company, and you are encouraged to hire them to complete necessary emergency services. And make no mistake about it; you may have hired this contractor to work for you, but his real customer is the insurance company. This is the old "chicken or the egg" analogy. In this relationship, you are the egg, and the insurance company is the chicken—and the chicken keeps laying these eggs.

So whose interests do you think are the most important to this contractor? He was brought there and/or referred by the insurance company for a reason—because he has shown himself to be a willing partner in helping the insurance company reduce its claim costs. If a dispute arises over whether or not a sofa can be cleaned, he will nearly always take the insurance adjuster's position. That is, unless he and the adjuster are working to gain your confidence in him, and then they may sacrifice an item or two, to show how he is really working for you—but be aware, and be skeptical.

While the use of these services is often necessary in order to prevent further damages, what you must realize is that by signing their blank work-authorization form, you have just given this contractor a blank check to spend your money. Worst yet is that most of these work-authorization forms include a direct-payment authorization, meaning that you have told your insurance company that it can pay these people directly out of your (money) claim proceeds.

Most people do not realize that it is not the insurance company's money at that point; it is *their* claim money that is being spent on these services. By signing a direct-payment authorization, you have just relinquished total control over your claim to this contractor. What often happens is that the emergency-services work turns into additional work, such as packing up all of the home's contents and removing them for storage and safekeeping while the structural damages are repaired.

By turning over control of the money, you have no recourse, should the contractor's work not be satisfactory. We recently had a relative who signed a direct-pay authorization after a serious water loss. After all of his personal property was returned, he found deep gouges in some of his furniture, a torn mattress cover, and many missing items. Because of the direct-payment authorization he had signed, this contractor was paid in full for his work, so it was a nightmare to negotiate a fair settlement of the damages, and then it was another three-month wait to get their refund check.

While many of these restoration services can be truly necessary, we often see restoration contractors spending tens of thousands of dollars of customers' claim money to inventory their property, wrap and pack it into boxes, and move it to a climate-controlled storage facility—property that, on day one, should have been identified as non-salvageable items. In layman's terms, this means that the property was a total loss and spending large sums of your money to pack it up in bubble wrap, move it to a climate-controlled storage warehouse, and pay exorbitant charges to store this property is a huge waste of your claim money. It is not uncommon for a pack-out/in on a residential claim to exceed $25,000, and on a commercial claim, it can be significantly more.

This really becomes a problem when your damages exceed your policy limits of coverage. It is not until then that consumers find that this wasted money could have been used to replace damaged property rather than be wasted at the insurance company's encouragement. Of course, the insurance company takes no responsibility for this waste of your money because it was your contractor, not theirs. Remember that blank work-authorization form you signed?

Moreover, we often find restoration contractors attempting to restore items that truly cannot be restored, and they get encouragement from the company adjuster because cleaning items is much cheaper than replacing them, and from the restoration company's perspective, they do not get paid for items that are not cleaned because they are a total loss. So there is an incentive for both the insurance company and the restoration company to attempt to clean everything, even truly uncleanable items.

Make no mistake about it: no matter how large or nationally known the restoration contractor is, they have a financial incentive to support the insurance companies' interests. It is a matter of survival.

Just recently, we represented a couple whose water-supply line to the toilet upstairs broke while they were out of town. When they got home, they found that the ceiling in their kitchen and family room had collapsed, and the house was full of water. When we arrived, the national emergency-services contractor was already on the scene doing the water extraction. After our inspection with an infrared camera to determine which areas had hidden water damage within the walls, we explained that we wanted all of these wet areas' drywall removed.

This started an argument with the restoration contractor, who insisted that these walls did not need to be removed and even suggested that wet drywall is actually stronger than new drywall because when it is dried out, it becomes harder. Even knowing our firm's credentials, he insisted upon getting the insurance company's adjuster's approval before he would remove these walls. Certainly, there can be no question as to who this national restoration contractor perceived to be his customer, and it surely was not the homeowner.

We recently represented a church that was encouraged by its insurance adjuster to hire a national restoration company to clean a huge portion of the building for smoke damage following a fire. This was done months before they hired us. By the time we were retained, this restoration contractor had racked up an incredible $870,000 in cleaning costs; they'd brought in workers from out of state and added their hotel rooms to their bill, along with massive amounts of overtime. To add insult to injury, the portion of the building that they had cleaned is now being required by the city's building department to be completely torn down.

This adjuster never investigated the status of this building with the city before recommending the expenditure of hundreds of thousands of dollars to clean a building that ultimately had to be demolished. And he never told the church that they did not have to engage this company in order to recover the money for the cleaning. The church staff surely could have put this money to better use if they had been given the proper advice, but both the insurance company adjuster and the restoration contractor were too busy worrying about their own interests to worry about the customers.

Also, be careful about relying upon restoration companies to take a physical inventory of your property. It is not their money, and many of the people these restoration companies hire are minimum-wage workers who couldn't care less about the accuracy of their listing. It takes a great deal of time and effort to prepare a proper and complete personal-property inventory. Over the years, we have found entire rooms that were accidentally left off these restoration contractor inventories and have reviewed inventories that did not provide adequate details and descriptions to competently evaluate the current replacement cost of the destroyed items.

If the item is not correctly described, it cannot be correctly priced for its current replacement-cost price. For instance, we recently handled a water-loss claim in Texas where the master-bedroom inventory included eighteen pairs of men's dress shoes that the insurance company priced at one hundred dollars per pair. After interviewing the insured, we discovered that most of these shoes were from Bruno Magli, Magnolini, and Metlan, with a couple pairs of Louis Vuitton shoes thrown in. These are all very expensive imported men's shoes with average values of more than $500 per pair. This is an example of how easily a bad item description can affect the value of the claim.

Now that we have covered the varying interests in your claim recovery by the insurance company, its adjuster, your agent, the restoration contractor, and the emergency-services restoration contractors, let's turn our attention to the claim process itself. After the insurance company has its emergency-restoration contractor busy extracting water and cleaning everything in sight, the next move is to develop a building-loss evaluation that is allegedly intended to restore your home or building to its pre-loss condition.

Unfortunately, more often than not, the insurance company's initial loss evaluations only account for a fraction of the actual costs required to restore your property. They offer you this quick, low-ball settlement check and hope that you will go away. It is our experience that the initial claim settlement offers, on average, are about 1/3 of the true value of loss. How can an insurance company's loss evaluations be so for off? It is by design!

This is how the program that was created by the business consultants at McKinsey is designed to work. They offer you a quick, low-ball claim settlement, and if you object to the amount, they put you through hell to get the balance of your rightful indemnity. They deliberately cause excessive delays in your claim's handling. Those who object to the company's claim payment are placed on the back burner and left to simmer for an extended period of time. Fighting a multibillion-dollar insurance company can be a daunting task, especially if you do not have the training and skills needed in order to win this negotiation.

During a recent litigation, we ran across a page from a major insurance company's training manual whereby they were teaching their adjusters to negotiate claims by using the "power of the checkbook." What they were saying was that the insurance company has the money in their bank account, and the customer who just had a loss needs this money in order to recover. So they instruct their adjusters to use their superior financial position to force a reduced settlement.

We use the word *negotiation* because that is essentially what an insurance claim is; a claim settlement is a negotiated settlement of estimated costs of repair. Most consumers have the misconception that a claim settlement is a finite number that can be calculated with exacting precision. They mistakenly believe that the insurance company's adjuster just needs to enter a few things into some computer program, and out comes the claim value. The fact is that a claim settlement is truly a negotiated estimate of the cost of repairs. If we were to have ten contractors or adjusters prepare their loss evaluation on the same claim, we would end up with ten different claim values.

How, then, does one determine what the correct value of a claim is? It comes down to understanding construction methods, looking critically at the operations that must be included in the loss evaluation, and confirming the prices for each of these operations. It also often requires making a judgment call on what reasonably is necessary to restore the property to its pre-loss condition. This is a highly technical process and one that takes years to learn. In fact, most contractors that do not do insurance restoration work do not understand how to use the computer software that is required by the insurance industry for claim evaluations.

A winning negotiation is the product of extensive construction experience, a vast knowledge of the estimating software, and an understanding of the coverages provided in the insurance policy. You have heard the saying "knowledge is power;" this could not be any truer than in the context of claim settlements.

Similarly, the negotiation of the claim settlement of personal or business property damages also requires training and expertise. Understanding cleaning techniques and understanding how smoke, heat, and water travel through a building during a fire and knowing how heat, smoke, and water can affect various types of finishes and materials takes years to learn. Understanding which items respond well to cleaning and which ones have little chance of being restorable is also important.

We often use a negotiating technique with insurance adjusters who are adamant that an item can be successfully cleaned. We tell them that we will allow them to test clean the item in dispute and if it does not clean to our satisfaction, they must pay the cost of cleaning from their claim-investigation budget and not from the policyholder's insurance proceeds. If there truly is a question on the cleanability of an item, we let the facts speak for themselves. Most often, they chose not to engage us in this claim "dance" and just agree to pay for the item.

These same issues also arise when working with dry-cleaning companies. They only get paid for cleaning items, so if they don't clean it, they don't get paid. This creates an incentive to attempt to clean items that there is no chance of salvaging. Insurance-company adjusters are more than willing partners to the dry cleaners because paying $2.50 to clean a shirt is much cheaper than paying forty-five dollars to replace it.

Don't be fooled by appearance! Many items can suffer hidden damage that may not be visible to the naked eye; e.g., electronic appliances may be harmed by the caustic acidity of soot and smoke that continues to damage electronic circuitry even after the item is allegedly cleaned and appears to be working fine. Fabrics (clothes, furniture, draperies) are subject to material deterioration from temperatures as low as 200 degrees. Even a small fire can quickly reach temperatures of 1,700 degrees, so beware of this issue. Mold, mildew, and other spore growths can occur inside walls and ceilings, which may result in health concerns for the occupants and can cause additional long-term damage to the structure.

The process of resolving your building or contents damages can go one of two ways. Either your adjuster is willing to compromise to the point of resolving your claim or he is not. It is not uncommon for the adjuster to throw you a bone, meaning that if he underpays the claim by thousands, he has tremendous latitude to offer some compromise amount to settle your claim. We recently had a commercial client that had repeatedly complained to the insurance company about the inadequacy of their settlement offer. By the time he was referred to us, he had had four different adjusters come out, each one giving him just a little bit more than the last. After our intervention, he recovered more than double the last adjuster's loss evaluation.

Most consumers go into the claims process ignorant of how this process really works and believing that insurance companies operate like other normal businesses. They blindly believe that insurance companies are honest business partners who make a promise and collect a policy premium, and in the event of a loss, they determine the fair value of the claim and issue a check. The reality is that many insurers have rigged the system so that their initial loss valuations are all substantially lower than the actual fair values of their consumer's claims. By low-balling every claim and making their customers fight for every dollar, they have dramatically increased their profit margins.

After a loss, it is not uncommon for you to place an undue amount of trust in your insurance company. When your home or your business has just been destroyed, it is quite natural to feel vulnerable and to feel hopeful that your insurer will do as it has promised. Most people find it hard to believe that a program like the one described here could exist in America. It truly is brilliantly shameful that the insurance industry has taken this approach to the settlement of claims, but this is, in fact, the new reality. These practices are here to stay because there is just too much money at stake, and to an insurance company, these additional profits are like crack to a drug addict.

Most insurance companies have moved to claims-management systems that take most of the discretion away from the field adjuster and place it in the hands of the claim manager or, in some cases, a committee of claims managers. This program is designed to control claims costs, and it makes the process of negotiating a fair settlement much more difficult and vastly more time-consuming. And time is not on the consumer's side. Remember, it is not the adjuster or his manager that are living in a hotel or in some temporary rental. It is not their business that has been interrupted, and it's not them who cannot fulfill their customer's orders. They get to go back to their homes every night after work without consequence. You, on the other hand, are the one who is inconvenienced and uncomfortable, and day-by-day, you become more motivated to settle your claim. They know this, and they now have you just where they want you.

Remember the three Ds: *delay, deny,* and *defend*! Welcome to the delay stage. But, do not despair. It is not impossible to obtain a fair claim settlement in a reasonable amount of time with tenacity and a knowledge of the game you are playing. A winning negotiation starts with a highly trained expert negotiator. If you are not up to the task yourself, then find people that you can really count on to support your claim. Your negotiated settlement will only be as good as your negotiator, so choose wisely.

CHAPTER FOUR

Rules of Appraisal and Other Alternative Resolution Methods

What happens when the two sides to the policy, you and your insurance company, cannot reach a settlement agreement on the claim? This is where the policy's appraisal clause comes in. Nearly all policies in America contain an appraisal clause, which is a mechanism for resolving a claim that is intended to be faster and less costly than litigation. An appraisal clause is simply an alternative dispute resolution method to resolve claims. If either you or the insurance company makes a demand for appraisal, participation in the process is mandatory in most cases and under certain circumstances.

Due to the extensive list of scenarios where submission to appraisal might be avoided, we will suggest that you seek the advice of an attorney for advice on your specific situation. What is most important to remember is that the appraisal clause was written *by* insurance companies, *for* insurance companies, so the odds of getting a truly fair settlement in this process are somewhat stacked against you.

One of the reasons for this is that insurance companies work daily on tens of thousands of claims and they control billions of dollars, so there are no shortages of appraisers willing to represent their interests. For the consumer, the list is much shorter, and truly qualified appraisers can be very difficult to find. However, with a reasonable amount of effort and critical verification of their qualifications, it is possible to find competent consumer appraisers.

Once you are satisfied that you have found a competent and experienced insurance appraiser, the first task in the appraisal process is usually for your appraiser and their appraiser to provide each other with disclosure statements setting forth their past and current relationships with their respective nominators. [15] Generally, the appraisal provision only requires that the appraisers be competent and disinterested. This means someone of reasonable intelligence, not necessarily an expert in the issues of dispute, and *disinterested* means that they have no financial interest in the outcome of the appraisal. This means that an appraiser generally cannot work on a contingency fee agreement, as this would make him interested in the outcome; however, there are certain exceptions to this rule. Check with an experienced insurance attorney for the rules in your jurisdiction.

The next step is for the appraisers to reach an agreement on a third person to serve as the umpire. If they cannot agree upon an umpire, they must submit a request to the nearest court having jurisdiction to have a judge appoint an umpire. The umpire is essentially the tie-breaker in the appraisal process. The umpire is nothing more than a third appraiser, and he actually is limited in his authority, as he only decides on items that the other two appraisers cannot agree upon.

In practice, however, umpires often exercise a great deal of authority over the appraisal process, as these people are usually retired judges or mediators/arbitrators who are used to being in control of the dispute-resolution process. Add to this the appraiser's fear of angering the umpire, which might lead him to rule against his nominator, and you have an alternative dispute-resolution system that does not actually function as it was intended.

Next, the two appraisers are instructed to conduct their inspections independent of each other and exchange their loss evaluations. They are then to meet in an attempt to reach agreement on as much of the loss as possible, and then, those items that are still in dispute are to be submitted to the umpire for a ruling. The intent of appraisal is that the umpire will decide upon one of the two positions of the appraisers placed before him.

---

[15]   Note: not all states require disclosure statements.

The appraisal award is final and binding upon both the consumer and the insurance company. Except under extremely rare circumstances involving fraud, collusion, or mistake, the courts will not generally overturn an appraisal award.

A host of problems have arisen with the manipulation of this dispute-resolution method. First and foremost is the problem with finding a good umpire who does not favor insurance companies. The insurance industry controls a tremendous amount of money and power and, by its nature, requires huge staffs of attorneys, both in-house counsel and outside counsel.

The sheer amount of legal work generated by insurance companies draws in many new lawyers looking for their first jobs out of law school. This creates significant numbers of attorneys who at least have somewhat of an insurance-defense background. Judges often come from the private-sector law firms; consequentially, a disproportionate number of judges and mediators also seem to have an insurance-defense background.

Throughout the years and in the many dozens of appraisals that our firm has been involved in, it has been our experience that the umpire candidates available tend to have a disproportionate number with backgrounds in insurance-defense work. This does not necessarily mean to say that these candidates cannot be unbiased in their judgments. In fact, some of the very best judges and even plaintiff attorneys we know started their careers as defense attorneys. Unfortunately, many have shown a certain amount of bias in favor of the insurance companies on some of our appraisals. It is no wonder, because if you do get an umpire on an appraisal who sides with the consumer on a significant dollar-value claim, it is possible that he may never be suggested or approved again to serve as an umpire for that insurer without a court appointment.

Also, most people do not realize how much insurance companies talk among themselves. Why would a person serving as an umpire want to make a ruling that would have the effect of eliminating him from consideration on any future insurance-related appraisal matters? Remember that this is how they make their living, so routinely ruling against insurance companies is the equivalent of biting the hand that feeds them. This elimination process is a significant disadvantage to a consumer looking to get fair treatment in the appraisal process, as the pool of qualified and unbiased umpires is constantly being wilted down to just "their guys."

As a consumer, it is extremely difficult to find good, competent, and unbiased appraisers and umpires, be they retired judges or professional mediators. The insurance industry has stacked the deck against customers' efforts to get a fair resolution of their claims.

The other problem with getting fair treatment in the appraisal process is one of the mindset of the umpire. Most judges or mediators are used to the idea of reaching a compromise agreement between the parties. This usually means "splitting the baby." This is not a big deal if both you and the insurance company are both working from reasonable positions on the value of loss or if you are both working from very unreasonable positions. Unfortunately, all too often, we go into this process with a realistic and honest evaluation, while the insurance company is stuck on an extremely low-ball estimate of damages. No matter how the umpire "splits the baby," the policyholder ends up with less than the fair value of his loss.

The way that appraisal is supposed to work is that the two appraisers each determine their loss evaluations separately and then meet to try to resolve their differences and reach an agreement on settlement of the appraisal. Any items that they cannot reach an agreement upon are to be submitted to the umpire for his ruling one way or the other. This process is intended to set the value of the claim. Unfortunately, the latest trend is for the insurance company's appraiser to refuse to agree on any items with our appraiser, thus placing all items of damage in the umpire's hands.

This significantly changes the entire appraisal process and usually leads to umpires who assume control of the appraisal as if they are still sitting on the bench as the judge. They exert a tremendous amount of influence in the appraisal because both appraisers are afraid to offend them, which could lead to an unfavorable result for their nominator. Lately, we are seeing umpires suggest their own compromise number somewhere in the middle of the two appraiser's evaluations, and then they attempt to get one or the other of the parties to agree with their position. Remember, an agreement by any two of the three appraisers is a binding settlement of the claim. Most often, this process has evolved into a process of "splitting the baby."

It is for this reason that we are not big fans of using the appraisal process to resolve a claim, generally speaking. We were taught that the appraisal was to be conducted as an open, honest process with the two appraisers reaching agreements on as many line items as possible and then submitting the disputed items only to the umpire. Then the umpire was to make a judgment on which appraiser's position was the most correct, given the loss situation.

Today's appraisal process looks nothing like it was designed to be. It has been many years since we have had an umpire actually take the time to go line by line through the appraiser's loss evaluations and decide the appraisal in this manner. Even though they are being paid by the hour, the umpires seem all too happy to take the shortcut of compromising on an arbitrary number, with little regard to the actual facts of the claim and the way in which the values for each restoration operation were determined. Some even reject evaluations prepared on the Xactimate estimating software over a contractor bid, even though the courts in the majority of the jurisdictions have ruled on this matter have found that the Xactimate software is sufficient proof as to the fair value of the costs of restoration.

Notwithstanding all of these problems with the appraisal process, there are circumstances where appraisal is still the best means to reach a resolution of the claim, and while it is far from a perfect process, it is still possible to get an acceptable result from appraisal, even though the odds are stacked against you. The individual circumstances of each claim differ and dictate whether or not this process is the best strategy for a successful—or at least, an acceptable—outcome.

Lately, we have seen a disturbing new trend by insurance companies. They may demand appraisal or agree to participate in an appraisal, and then they try to limit what damages are the subject of appraisal and which cannot be ruled upon by the appraisal panel. You see, under the rules of appraisal, issues that involve a question of the policy's coverage for damages are not within the scope of the appraisal process, and these issues are strictly prohibited from being addressed by the appraisal panel. The appraisal process is designed to only determine the value of the loss in the event of a dispute.

In most cases, it is extremely difficult if not impossible to separate the value of the loss from the scope of repair or the cause of the damages. Insurance companies are trying to restrict the scope of the appraisal process by asserting that not all of the damages being claimed are the result of the covered loss being claimed or that the determination of the proper scope of repair is not a function of the valuation of the loss, but is a coverage matter for the courts to decide. Because in most jurisdictions, appraisers are not allowed to decide how the damages occurred, but only the value of the loss, this places the consumer at an unfair disadvantage by making the appraisal process irrelevant to resolving the dispute. Even after the appraisal is concluded, the consumer could still be forced to litigate the coverage issues on whether the damages claimed qualify for coverage under the policy. Using coverage as a tool, insurance companies can limit the scope of the appraisal and thus reduce the ultimate cost of the claim.

There have recently been some encouraging new court rulings which address these arbitrary limitations to the appraisal process. The issue on the authority of appraisers to address "causation" of damages has been the source of recent litigation in Arizona, and it has been addressed in other states as well, with very different results. Arizona, which has a history of favoring alternative dispute-resolution methods, gives a certain amount of discretion to the appraisal panel to decide if the damages are the result of the covered loss. Also, recent trends in Colorado law have also given us new hope that appraisers will be afforded the authority to determine the cause of loss and the scope of repairs within the appraisal process. Yet, other states continue to have more restrictive views on the authority of appraisers. If you encounter this situation, we suggest you find an experienced bad-faith attorney who is familiar with the laws of your state.

Insurance companies are now using coverage issues, or more correctly, *misusing* coverage issues more and more often to limit the basis for the appraisal panel to make their loss determination and to obtain more favorable appraisal decisions. Insurance companies and their coverage attorneys are experts in separating you from your money. This practice is the second *D*, as in *deny*, in the three Ds.

Your only other option in these situations is to take what you can get through appraisal or litigate your claim. Of course, litigation is not an easy process, and it is not a quick resolution to your situation. Time is on the insurance companies' side, not yours. It can take eighteen months or more to get your case before a jury on a bad-faith insurance-claim litigation. Not many people have the stamina and fortitude to make this trek, and insurance companies know this, which is why this third *D* stands for Defend in their program.

Finding a qualified bad-faith attorney to take on an insurance company for smaller dollar amounts can be very difficult—or impossible. This is why insurance companies seem even more emboldened on the smaller claims. Hiring an attorney on an hourly basis is generally cost prohibitive unless you are independently wealthy, in which case you would probably not waste your time with this anyway. Attorneys' fees on an hourly basis could easily exceed $50,000 by the time the case is ready for trial, not to mention the costs of hiring experts and other litigation costs. The only reasonable option most people have is to find someone willing to handle their case on a contingency-fee basis. But, as mentioned above, it is hard to find a good attorney to take on a claim with a small amount in dispute, as the cap on punitive damages that was imposed by the ruling in *Campbell* makes these cases unprofitable to litigate, from a business standpoint.

Winning in litigation requires the perfect combination of facts, a very well-documented claim file, credible experts, a very experienced attorney, a tremendous amount of patience, and a great deal of luck. Even if you win big, expect the insurance company to appeal the decision, so you will go through another year or more and possibly another trial to get a final resolution to your claim. This is not an easy process, and the deck is stacked against the policyholder. But it is not impossible to persevere and get justice. We do it every day for our clients.

It is important to remember that most cases settle before trial. Most courts make mediation mandatory before a case may proceed to trial. This alternative dispute method helps to give closure and finality to both sides in a disputed claim. Often, the certainty of a mediated settlement, if it is enough, is better than the uncertainty of an award by a jury. If your case is solid and well-prepared, and if your attorney has done a good job of creating risk for the insurance company through discovery and through various motions to the court, there is a good chance that the insurance company's legal counsel will, at some point in the litigation process, recommend that the insurance company settle the case.

Insurance companies know that most jurors are not sympathetic to insurance companies. If the plaintiff is perceived to be a good witness and the plaintiff attorney has created risk, a fair settlement is possible. Insurance companies are expert in evaluating risk. If your attorney does a good job of preparing your case through motions to the court, the testimonies of great expert witnesses, and an extensive discovery process, it is likely that you can achieve a reasonable settlement sometime before trial.

There is one final alternative-dispute method that we will not spend much time on; it is rarely used in insurance disputes. This method is known as arbitration. Arbitration is a dispute-resolution method that places the settlement in the control of a panel of arbitrators. A settlement under this process is final and binding upon the parties, which is generally not an attractive alternative to a courtroom in most cases. Submission of a claim dispute to arbitration is generally voluntary and happens only with the consent of the parties. In our twenty-three years in adjusting, we have never had a case submitted to arbitration, if that gives you a sense of how rare this method is used in insurance disputes on first-party claims.

Whether your claim is resolved through appraisal or mediation, the result will likely be a compromise on what you believe to be the true value of your claim. Insurers will sometimes demand appraisal when they know they have exposure for damages, as this is a way of resolving the claim by paying less than the full value of loss. Consumers should avoid this process if at all possible, as it most often favors insurance companies. However, under the right circumstances, appraisal can provide a path to a practical resolution of your claim and in a reasonable amount of time.

CHAPTER FIVE

"But I Thought I Bought a Replacement-Cost Policy"

Insurance policies have evolved over the years from the simple "fire only" policies of the past into the more recent "risks of direct loss" policies that are most common today. Insurance companies have expanded their policy coverages to meet consumer demands, and premium revenues increase with these creative offerings. What customers would not want full replacement-cost recovery if they suffered a loss to their home or business? Yet, as the old saying goes, the devil is in the details.

While there are some replacement-cost policies that pay the full replacement cost up front, these policies are rare and usually come at a significantly increased cost. The majority of replacement-cost policies fall into a different category because, while they do pay full replacement cost under a prescribed set of circumstances, there are hoops that you must jump through in order to obtain these policy benefits.

When you bought your policy, your insurance agent probably assured you that you were buying "full replacement-cost coverage for your home or business and your personal property." What he probably left out is that the insurance company is going to make you jump through all sorts of hoops in order to actually obtain these "replacement-cost" policy benefits. We do not wish to cast doubt upon your agent's intentions, but the fact is, very few agents take the time to really explain to their customers how these replacement-cost policies work at the time the policy is purchased. Most consumers discover for the first time after a loss event that certain steps must be taken to obtain the full replacement-cost benefits suggested by the policy.

By up-selling consumers on replacement-cost coverage, the insurance company earns an additional premium for the policy, and when customers are faced with the reality of what it takes to recover the full replacement cost for their claim, many are not willing to play the game and simply take what they can get without all the hoop jumping. Unfortunately, from our experience, very few claimants ever actually recover the full replacement-cost policy benefits that are recoverable without professional assistance. Unless your claim is a total loss or you are diligent in documenting and submitting the replacement receipts for your property, it is unlikely that you will ever see the full replacement cost benefits that you were sold. There are those claims where the actual cash value of the loss exceeds the policy limits of coverage. In these cases, the limits of the coverage would be paid.

Many times, we have reviewed insurance claims where the homeowner had driven all over town buying discounted building materials and negotiating with various subcontractors to get the very best price for repairs, only to find that all of their efforts only resulted in reducing the insurance company's obligation to them for the replacement-cost benefits.

You might ask, "How is this possible? How can the insurer sell me a promise of replacement-cost coverage and then give me something less?" The answer lies in the wording of the policy's "loss settlement" provision, which is where these "hoops" and qualifiers are located. Most of today's insurance policies contain stipulations in the loss-settlement provision that restrict the insurance company's initial obligation for payment on the loss to the actual cash value (ACV) of loss, until repair or replacement is completed. You may or may not know what the term *actual cash value* means, but simply put, it is the depreciated value of the item lost or damaged after reductions for its current age and condition.

What this means is that you receive only the actual cash value (depreciated) payment up front, and the insurance company withholds the depreciation portion until a receipt is produced to prove the item has been replaced.

On personal-property coverage, most policies promise to settle the claim on a replacement-cost basis, but for no more than the smallest of the following:

1) The actual cash value;
2) The fair-market value;
3) The stated limit or other limit of insurance under this policy that applies to the property; or
4) The amount actually and necessarily spent to repair or replace damage to the property.

In other words, you only get the actual cash value, i.e., the depreciated value of the property, up front. If the actual amount spent is less than the replacement-cost amount that was agreed to by the insurance company, you get the lesser of these amounts. It does not seem that complicated until you start replacing everything in your home or business and try to match up all the receipts with the listing of the personal-property items. And what happens when an item that is replaced is not exactly like the one that was destroyed? What if the item lost is no longer available for purchase? Will the insurance company allow you to substitute one item for another? These are just some of the reasons why very few homeowners ever receive the full policy benefits, and this is why the policy is written this way.

To begin with, the policy's requirements run directly in conflict with human nature. Everyone wants to get a good deal. Nobody wants to pay full retail price for something. People want to negotiate a discount; they want a deal. Negotiating may be good when you're buying a car, but on an insurance claim, it may not ultimately benefit your situation. If you manage to negotiate a lower price with your contractor for the repair of your home, the party that benefits from your efforts will probably be the insurance company. All you have done is spend your time and energy to lower their obligation for payment of your claim.

Furthermore, insurance companies know that no one is going to replace every item in his or her home or business in the event of a major loss. So, by structuring the replacement-cost recovery in this manner, they can sell you replacement insurance coverage at a higher premium, while rarely ever having to pay the full replacement-cost policy benefits promised. When they sell you the policy, most agents do not explain what you must do to obtain the replacement-cost benefits in the event of a loss. They just assure you that you have full replacement-cost coverage. While this may be reassuring, it can be somewhat deceptive by omission.

We do not want to throw all of the good and well-meaning agents under the bus on this issue. Some of them may not truly understand how the policy is applied in a loss situation, and one can argue that explaining every aspect of coverage to a customer before a loss is not reasonable when selling an insurance policy. But, by referencing their policies as a "replacement-cost policies," the insurance companies are creating an expectation in consumers' minds that, in reality, is not exactly true.

Maybe it would be better if they called these policies "qualifying replacement-cost policies" so as to emphasize that a customer must take certain steps to obtain the replacement-cost benefits. It would be more appropriate to make this provision known at the time their policy is sold. Instead, they hide the qualifying language deep within the dozens of pages of the policy. Or maybe insurers should place the replacement-cost requirements on the front page of the policy in sixteen-point type?

How is it possible that insurers are allowed to get away with this? The answer lies in the application of the law as it is applied in most courtrooms. Also, we can look to state statutes or to the regulations of the various state departments of insurance.

Under the law, the courts will generally interpret contract provisions by assigning them their plain and simple means. Unless the provision is subject to more than one reasonable interpretation or it violates some law, insurance contracts are generally given their strict meaning and construction by the courts. In other words, you are bound by the language in the policy unless you can prove that you were misled by the agent.

State statutory law is another place to look for modification to the insurance policy, as state statutes usually supersede the policy language. So if you are lucky enough to live in a state that has a statute that requires the insurance company to pay the full replacement-cost value of a claim up front, regardless of the policy's verbiage, you may be entitled to receive the full replacement-cost benefits of the policy. Also, if you live in a state that has a valued policy law and you have a qualifying total loss, you may be entitled to receive the full replacement-cost benefits of the policy without having to justify every expenditure.

Furthermore, state insurance regulatory agencies, usually referred to as the Department of Insurance, may exercise some regulatory control over the policy language and the language of all insurance coverage documents. In some states, before insurers can issue or revise a policy or insert a new policy provision, they must first get approval from the Department of Insurance. Unfortunately, many regulatory agencies, due, in part, to budget cuts, have gone to a policy of letting insurers write what they wish, and they only step in if an issue of concern is brought to their attention. Many state agencies do not even review the policy documents; they just stamp them as "received" and file them, leaving the consumers to find their own remedies in the courtrooms.

Another condition that must be met in order to qualify for full replacement coverage on many policies is that the amount of insurance on the dwelling at the time of loss must equal or exceed the percentage stated under the building coverage's coinsurance percentage amount. For example, say the dwelling's replacement-cost value at the time of loss is $100,000 and the coinsurance provision requires you to insure the dwelling to 80 percent. If your coverage limit on the dwelling is less than $80,000, you may incur a penalty, which is deducted from your claim proceeds. This issue is discussed more fully in a later chapter.

Also, under some of today's policies, certain types of property may not be eligible for replacement-cost coverage. Items such as fences, decks, carpeting, awnings, household appliances, outdoor antennas, and outdoor equipment are some of the types of items that are often covered only for their actual cash value, even under a replacement-cost policy.

Finally, under most homeowners' policies, the insured may choose to settle the loss on an actual-cash value-basis, and he or she may later make a claim for the replacement-cost value. Most policies require that the policyholder provide the insurance company notification of their intent to make a claim for the replacement-cost benefits within 180 days. While the policies are often silent as to how the 180-day period is calculated, if at all possible, we recommend using the date of loss as the trigger for this provision. This will help avoid trouble. If the claim process extends beyond the 180-day time limit before a settlement is reached, don't assume that you have forfeited your rights to the replacement-cost recoveries. Make your claim immediately, and if you get pushback, consult with an attorney, as most states have laws that toll (delay) these types of forfeiture provisions.

Additionally, most policies require that repairs or restoration be completed before the insurance company is obligated to issue payment. We are starting to see new policies that now include provisions that limit recovery for restorations completed to only restorations that are completed within twelve months of the date of loss. We have also seen policies that require repairs to be completed within two years.

There are good legal arguments to be made and intervening factors to consider regarding the way in which these policy provisions might be applied to your specific claim, but we would suggest that you try to avoid problems as much as possible by trying to work within the timeframes allowed under your policy. Try as best you can to complete the restoration within the policy's required period. If that is not possible, write to the insurer asking for their written agreement to extend this time period. If they give you extra time, be sure that you have their agreement in writing. If they decline your request, consult with experienced insurance attorney to better understand your rights under the laws of your state.

The bottom line is that these policies provide full replacement-cost coverage only if you incur this cost. So rather than running all over town trying to find ways to reduce your restoration costs, it might make more sense to use a qualified general contractor and let them do all the running for you. After all, that is what they are being paid for, and you may not be entitled to these additional benefits anyway. So save yourself a lot of time and aggravation; hire a qualified professional, and use the policy benefits to their full advantage. An insurance policy is not designed to put money in your pocket, but to restore you to the position you were in before the loss. At the end of the day, that is what you should be striving for as well.

We have recently seen an increase in denials of coverage for repairs or personal-property replacements that were not completed within the policy's stated time periods. Generally speaking, the courts have traditionally frowned upon these types of forfeiture clauses, but that has not stopped insurance companies from invoking these clauses to deny the full recovery of policy benefits. We recently had a major insurance company delay the consumer's first claim payment on their total-loss house fire for more than nine months, and then, when the restoration was completed, one year and three months after the date of loss, the insurance company refused to issue payment of the depreciation holdback on a replacement-cost policy.

The English courts, as far back as the mid-seventeenth century, created a rule of equity against the arbitrary forfeiture of contract rights under the theory that such forfeitures were unduly harsh. Our court system today continues to disfavor such a draconian penalty as the forfeiture of insurance benefits in insurance contracts. While the policy sets forth specific limitations on the recovery of specific policy benefits, few courts will allow such a draconian penalty as the complete forfeiture of the contract benefits.

Notwithstanding, if you can comply with the policy's time limits for making claim for replacement-cost benefits, by all means, make every attempt to do so. If the time period has expired and the insurance company refuses to accept the replacement-cost claim, you should seek that advice of an insurance attorney because there is a good chance you may prevail on this issue.

CHAPTER SIX

Recovering Contractor's Overhead and Profit

We were recently contacted by a local restoration contractor, who asked us if insurance companies are required to pay for contractor's overhead and profit on a claim settlement. The contractor had several claims with the same insurance company, but it had refused to pay the traditionally accepted contractor fees for overhead and profit (O&P), leaving him thousands of dollars short on these restoration projects. This is one of the more common deceptive claims practices that we encounter in our everyday claims handling.

It is not as if, at this point, there is any question about the fact that insurance companies are responsible for these legitimate contractor fees. Does the insurance company owe for contractor's overhead and profit on their building damages analysis? This issue has been addressed in courtrooms across the country on numerous occasions over the last two decades, and the answers provided by the courts are a resounding *yes*!

This wrongful-claims practice of deducting contractor overhead and profit was addressed by the court as far back as 1982 in the Arizona Supreme Court case of *Zuckerman vs. Transamerica Ins. Co.* Although that case's dispute originated over the O&P issue, it was the forfeiture clause that was eventually brought before the Supreme Court. However, the court did address the O&P issue via Supreme Court Justice Feldman's specific footnote on page 141, marked by **, which states: "The company's

(Transamerica's) position is dubious on this point. The policy contains no clause permitting such deductions from the amount of loss. It does provide that the company 'does ensure' Zuckerman 'to the extent of the actual cash value of the property …'" (emphasis supplied.)[16]

But insurance companies can be very persistent when it comes to reducing claims payments and increasing profits. So this again became an issue in 1994, in a class-action lawsuit that was filed in Pennsylvania over State Farm's practice of routinely deducting amounts for contractor overhead and profit, in addition to depreciation from their replacement-cost estimates to determine the actual cash value claim payment. The court, in *Gilderman v. State Farm Ins.*, 649 A.2d 941 (Pa. Super. 1994), ruled as follows: "We hold that repair or replacement costs include any cost that an insured is reasonably likely to incur in repairing or replacing a covered loss."[17]

This reasoning was followed a few years later in the state of Michigan in *Salesin v. State Farm Fire & Cas.*[18] Since that time, this issue has been subject to class-action lawsuits in several other jurisdictions, including Texas and Oklahoma. This issue was also the subject of discussion in an August 2000 insurance-industry article written in *Claims Magazine*. In this article, the author laid out the reasoning behind inclusion and exclusion of contractor O&P payments under an insurance policy. The author concludes that insurance adjusters should consider the circumstances as outlined in the *Gilderman* and *Salesin* courts' rulings, stating: "Under this view, overhead and profit are assumed to have gone into the property when it was new. The insured is considered to have some of that value left at the time of loss, and loss of that value should be considered part of the damage suffered by the insured."[19]

In 2006, the Arizona Court of Appeals ruled, in *Tritschler v. Allstate*, as follows: "If the cost to repair or replace the damaged property would likely require the services of a general contractor, the contractor's overhead and

16   Zuckerman vs. Transamerica Ins. Co., 650 P.2d 441 (Ariz. 1982)
17   Gilderman v. State Farm Ins. Co., 649 A.2d 941 (Pa. Super. 1994)
18   Salesin v. State Farm Fire & Cas., 581 N.W.2d 781 (Mich. Ct. App. 1998)
19   *Claims Magazine* August 2000

profit fees should be included in determining actual cash value, even when an insured ultimately elects to complete personally the needed repairs."[20]

And just recently, the Florida Supreme Court, in its July 2013 decision in *Trinidad v. Florida Peninsula*,[21] left no doubt that this wrongful reduction of policy benefits will not be tolerated in Florida. The court ruled that homeowners are entitled to recover the full cost of replacement, whatever that includes, and whether or not the repair or reconstruction actually takes place.[22]

You might ask yourself, with similar rulings like these all over the country, why would insurance companies continue to engage in this wrongful claims-handling practice? The answer is simple: it is all about the money. With a 20 percent savings on every claim payout, the money is just too enticing for many insurance companies. Insurance companies count on the fact that most people do not know their rights under an insurance policy, so they are easy marks for being shortchanged in their purchase of insurance coverage. And because most people do not seek professional help when they have a claim, they are left to rely upon the integrity of their insurance company. This is a recipe for disaster.

Insurance companies are meant to perform an actuarial analysis to try to make their money by taking policy-premium payments in exchange for a promise of coverage, should a covered loss event happen. Insurance companies keep careful records of past loss events, and they are quite good at predicting future events as well. These actuarial records are not only effective for predicting the number of loss events in a given year; they are also effective for analyzing the insurer's exposure to liabilities created by the filing of a lawsuit. It is a fact that very few claimants will go to the trouble and the expense of hiring an attorney if they feel they are being treated unfairly on a claim. Some estimate this number to be much less than 5 percent of all claimants. Also, of the few claimants who choose to sue, less than 5 percent of them will ever see the inside of a courtroom, as the majority will settle sometime before trial.

---

20 Tritschler v. Allstate, 144 P.3d 519 (Ariz. App. 2006)

21 Trinidad v. Florida Peninsula Insurance Co., 99 So. 3d 502, 504 (Fla. 3d DCA 2011)

22 *Remodeling* November 2013

To better explain how this tactic works, let's put some hypothetical numbers to this theory, so as to get a better understanding of how this all works. For the purposes of this example, let's assume that an insurer will suffer 1,000 fire claims in a given year, with an average-sized claim of $100,000 before application of contractor's O&P; this means that, on average, if the insurer does not pay contractor's O&P, it will save a total of $20,000 (or 20 percent) of the damages per claim.

If this insurance company refuses to pay contractor's overhead and profit on all of these claims, we can assume that a certain number of customers will not take this lying down and will file suit against the insurer. Using the litigation-probability data from past experience, this means that less than 5 percent of the claimants, or approximately fifty of them, will actually file suit against the insurance company. Of these, less than 5 percent will actually stay with it all the way to a jury trial, meaning that there will only be two or three trials that result from such blatantly wrongful conduct.

Remember, the US Supreme Court's ruling in *Campbell* reduced the penalties for getting caught for intentional bad-faith claims practices to a factor of a single-digit multiplier of the contract damages claimed, i.e., less than ten times the amount. So here, the claimant's contract damages average $20,000. Using the *Campbell* ruling as a guideline, the most that the court can award for punitive damages is $180,000, or nine times the contract damages, plus, of course, the $20,000 that it should have paid in the first place.

Assuming that the insurance company loses all three trials, its exposure is a total of just $540,000 in punitive damages, plus the $60,000 in contract damages it should have paid in the beginning.

Now, let's compare this payout to the money the insurance company would have saved on all of the other claims where it withheld contractor's overhead and profit. There were 950 of the 1,000 claimants that did not file a lawsuit, but instead stood by and took what was offered to settle their claim. On these claims, the insurance company saved $19 million; yes, that is right—nineteen million dollars.

Then there are still the other forty-seven people who filed lawsuits but settled their cases before trial. For these claimants, let's assume that their attorneys were successful in getting the insurance company to pay the contractor's overhead and profit, and they got them to pay an additional $20,000 for the attorney's fees and costs. These costs would total $940,000, plus the wrongfully withheld amounts, totaling another $940,000.

To summarize, the net savings for the insurance company engaged in this blatantly improper conduct is roughly $16.5 million dollars. The math works as follows: there was the initial $20,000 per claim withheld, which the insurance company eventually was forced to pay on the fifty claims that filed suit, which totals $1 million. Now add to this the extra settlement costs for the forty-seven people who settled their claims before litigation; this totals approximately another $940,000. Lastly, we must add the amounts awarded in the three trials that resulted from this wrongful conduct, which total $540,000. So in doing the math, we have $1 million, plus $940,000, plus $540,000, for a total insurer cost of $2,480,000. This example only considered 1,000 claims. Imagine how much money is at stake when you apply this practice to the actual number of claims that an insurance company handles each year.

If we were to give you $19 million dollars, would you be willing to give us $2.5 million of it back? Only paying out to those who recognize that this practice is wrong can certainly pay huge dividends. There can be no other explanation for the same insurance company that has lost on this issue in the courts to still be engaging in this wrongful-claims practice. And it is even clearer now why that company is one of those in the top ten of the Consumer Reports listing of the worst insurance companies.[23]

When your insurance company sends its loss evaluation to you, you need to look at the last couple of pages to see if contractor's overhead and profit is included in their evaluation. To help you better understand what to look for, please see Figure #1 below, which shows a properly calculated loss evaluation. Then compare it to Figure #2, which shows how insurers oftentimes prepare their loss evaluations to exclude the contractor overhead and profit costs they should be paying.

---

[23]   *Consumer Reports* May 2014

Figure #1 – Depicts the correct manner of preparing a loss evaluation[24]

Summary for Dwelling

Line Item Total			954,188.74
Total Adjustments for Base Service Charges			789.10
Material Sales Tax		9.446%	28,377.88
Storage Rental Tax	@	9.446%	25.28
Subtotal			983,381.00
Overhead	@	10.00%	98,338.10
Profit	@	10.00%	98,338.10
Replacement Cost Value			1,180,057.20
Less Depreciation			(133,843.12)
Actual Cash Value			1,046,214.08
Net Claim			1,046,214.08
Total Recoverable Depreciation			133,843.12
Net Claim if Depreciation is Recovered			1,180,057.20

Figure#2 – Depicts the improper exclusion of contractor overhead and profit

Summary for Dwelling

Line Item Total			693,84.50
Storage Rental Tax	@	6.140%	42,601.99
Replacement Cost Value			$736,445.49
Less Depreciation			(133,360.11)
Actual Cash Value			$623,085.38
Less Depreciation			(5,000.00)
Net Claim			$618,085.38
Total Recoverable Depreciation			113,360.11
Net Claim if Depreciation is Recovered			$731,445.49

As you can see from these two examples, the exclusion of contractor's overhead and profit makes a significant impact on the total amount of a claim recovery. But this is not the only way that insurers squeeze out extra profits from your claim. Be sure to double check the math on their loss evaluations, as it is not uncommon for an insurance company to pay contractor's overhead and profit on only certain portions of the claim, rather than on the entirety of the loss.

---

[24] From actual estimates prepared on Xactware estimating software

We often encounter insurers who calculate contractor overhead and profit, excluding some of the repairs that are called out in their evaluations. On an active litigation matter, we found an insurer who had excluded the cost of roofing from its calculation of contractor overhead and profit. Their explanation for this reduction thus far has been somewhat murky, but with critical depositions in the next couple of weeks, we will likely flesh it out.

Contractor's overhead and profit amounts are not the only omissions that we routinely find on insurance-company loss evaluations. Other typical exclusions include some of the other contractor services that are required to complete the restoration of your property, such as building permits, fence rental fees, crane rental, and environmental remediation (with issues such as asbestos).

One of the insurance industry's favorite practices is to exclude the payment of contractor's overhead and profit on the payment for the cost of building permits. If your adjuster has done this on your claim, suggest that he drive downtown to the city's building and planning department and sit in the waiting area for the plans check desk for hours to get the building permit issued to begin reconstruction. It is absurd to believe that this task does not require significant time and effort, and do not be fooled by his explanation that this cost is included with the payment of overhead and profit on the other portion of the claim.

In the restoration-estimating software known as Xactimate, which is the most widely used insurance-estimating tool, there is a button that you can click that provides a detailed explanation of exactly what services are included in the line-item description. For the line item pertaining to the cost of obtaining a building permit, contractor's overhead and profit should be paid as an additional cost, to compensate the contractor for his time in obtaining the proper permits.

Likewise, insurance companies sometimes exclude contractor's overhead and profit from the costs for the rental of a crane or other heavy equipment. Simply put, why should the contractor spend his time securing the necessary heavy equipment to make the repairs and not receive compensation for his time?

Another trade that is most often excluded from contractor's overhead and profit is asbestos or mold abatement. It is quite common for insurers to exclude this cost, primarily because these costs can be very high and they require the services of a properly trained and licensed abatement contractor. If the general contractor has any involvement with the hiring or scheduling of the abatement contractor, it is entirely proper to pay the general contractor for his overhead and profit on the abatement work.

These are just some of the more common examples of the manipulations that insurance companies so often make when determining the actual cash value of a claim. There are as many potential wrongful reductions to your loss evaluation as there are creative claims adjusters and claims managers. The key is to be diligent in reviewing the claim evaluation and hold your insurance company accountable for the full value of your loss.

CHAPTER SEVEN

Misapplication of Depreciation

The use of depreciation can significantly impact consumers' ultimate recovery for their loss, just as the intentional misuse of depreciation can. This is one of those areas of insurance that is so complex that many insurance adjusters do not even truly understand the proper methods for determining the correct amount to depreciate your property. So, then, how can a consumer know whether or not he or she is being treated fairly by the insurance company in the settlement of a claim? Add to this the fact that even knowing how to use depreciation properly still leaves a great deal that is subject to opinion or speculation and you have created a system that encourages abusive claims-handling practices.

It is a fact that the improper use of depreciation is one of the most abused of all the insurance claim processes. It is likely this way because the subjective nature of applying depreciation insulates the insurance company significantly from accusations of bad-faith claims-handling conduct. This is because it can be extremely difficult to prove that the adjuster's application of excessive depreciation to the damaged property was intentionally designed to underpay the claim and not just a mistake in judgment.

Not to get too involved in the legal processes that govern insurance bad-faith law, but, generally speaking, if a consumer wishes to file litigation against an insurance company alleging bad-faith claims handling, he must prove that the insurance company was deliberate in its abuse of the valuation process and not simply mistaken or grossly negligent. This can be difficult to prove in regards to something that is as subjective as the application of depreciation to damaged real property, personal property or business personal property items.

Also, because consumers are not trained in the proper application of depreciation and because the methods used are not actually spelled out in the policy, it is nearly impossible for a consumer to know if he or she is being mistreated. The lack of knowledge of the proper application of depreciation increases the likelihood that the misuse of the depreciation valuation process will become epidemic. The fact is that in most claims that we are asked to review, insurers left on their own appear to apply excessive amounts of depreciation to both structure losses and on personal-property items.

You might ask why an insurance company would do this. The answer is elementary: the less money that they pay out initially, the less ability that consumers have to replace all of their damaged property. And the more hoops they erect for customers to jump through to discourage recovery of this additional depreciation holdback indemnity, the less likely the customers will be to make these claims. The fact is that these policy provisions are cleverly constructed to give the insurance company the upper hand and to improve their corporate net profits. They know that no one will replace everything in their home or business in the event of a major loss. And what you don't replace, you lose the depreciation holdback on.

You are sold an insurance policy with assurances that it includes full replacement-cost coverage; yet, most claimants never get the full benefits of the policy's promise of coverage. As mentioned in the previous chapter, we believe that this process defies the policyholders' reasonable expectations of insurance coverage, and we do not believe that an insurer should be allowed to sell a replacement-cost policy without making the exact terms of the replacement agreement crystal clear to the buyer.

Depreciation is applicable to both your personal and business property as well as to your real property (buildings). The rules of application are essentially the same for both real property and personal property. Depreciation is designed to account for the age of an item, its use, and the possible obsolescence of the damaged property to create a current street value for the item as it was at the time of the loss. This is what is referred to as the actual cash value of the property. There are three primary tests for the measurement of actual cash value used by the courts. You will need to find out which test your state uses through your own research or through the help of attorney.

In some jurisdictions, the actual cash value of property is defined as replacement cost less depreciation, which is the current replacement cost of the damaged item, minus a depreciation amount to account for the age and wear and tear of the item.

Other states recognize "fair market value" as the test of actual cash value. Fair market value is defined as the price that property would realize in a marketplace of willing buyers and sellers, acting in their own interests, within a reasonable period of time. In those states that recognize this method for determination of actual cash value, it has produced mixed results and confusion, primarily due to the differences between the application of this method by state law and the methods set forth in most insurance contracts, which define actual cash value as replacement cost less depreciation. There have been instances where creative insurance companies have been able to use fair-market-value laws to exploit the valuation process to the detriment of their policyholders.

The majority of state courts in the United States recognize the "Broad Evidence Rule" as the standard by which insurers are to determine the cash value of destroyed property. Under the Broad Evidence Rule, an insurance company cannot rely solely upon the two traditional methods of *market value* or *replacement cost value minus depreciation* as the exclusive methods for value determination. Under the Broad Evidence Rule, these traditional methods can be used as guidelines, but the insurance company must give due consideration to every fact and circumstance that would logically lead to a correct value of the damaged or destroyed property.

This rule requires that a thorough examination be made of every standard of value that might have a bearing on the property being considered. Some of these standards include:

- The age of the item
- The use factor

- The obsolescence of the property
- The profit likely to accrue from the property
- The property's tax value
- The replacement cost
- The condition of the property
- The location
- The market value
- The original cost
- Offers to buy or sell

Then there are a few states that have not weighed in definitively as to the recognized method for determining actual cash value. While state laws vary on the methods of valuation, most insurance companies use the method set forth in the insurance policy of replacement cost value minus depreciation to determine the actual cash-value payments. It has been our experience that nearly all insurance companies consider only the useful life (age) of the items in making their determination of value, even in the states that follow the Broad Evidence Rule. Few insurers take into consideration the type of property being evaluated, and most have very punishing and often unreasonable depreciation schedules.

We have seen insurers take 60 percent depreciation on a six-year-old set of metal storage shelves. In our off-site file storage, we have metal shelving units that we bought more than fifteen years ago that still work just as well as they did the day we bought them. We have had an insurance company depreciate a one hundred-year-old antique oak desk by 90 percent. Antiques, by their nature, generally do not decrease in value as they get older, but in fact become even more valuable with age. This is the nature of an antique. On other occasions, we have seen insurers apply depreciation to items that were new and unopened at the time of loss, simply because an insured listed the item as six months old, such as Christmas presents purchased early.

In the insurance industry's claims-training textbooks, adjusters are trained to use the Broad Evidence Rule in making their determination of actual cash values. One such textbook, *Property Loss Adjusting* by James Markham, gives an example of how the use of a sofa can affect its value. In this example, the author explains that a five-year-old sofa in the living room of a family with six kids and a dog would probably show far more wear than the same sofa in the living room of an elderly retired couple.[25]

This same criteria can be applied to a three-year-old men's business suit. If it is worn by a banker who wears suits every day for work, it is likely to exhibit far more wear than a suit owned by a retired gentlemen who only wears a suit once or twice a year to special functions. In this scenario, the older gentleman's suit could easily last ten or fifteen years and would surely not depreciate as quickly as the banker's suit.

Notwithstanding this training that adjusters should have received and the state laws that regulate property valuation, insurers use punishing depreciation schedules that are designed to significantly underpay the actual cash value of the damaged property. This is probably the most prominent deceptive claims practice that we encounter. The insurance industry does not consider the use of your property or its condition at the time of loss. They base their loss evaluations upon archaic depreciation schedules, such as various government depreciation tables, which were never designed for application to property-insurance claims valuation and significantly understate the useful life of the damaged property. They then rely upon the age of the item as the sole determination of its current actual cash value.

To better illustrate how this might affect the average homeowner, let's assume that you had a total-loss house fire and that the total replacement-cost value of your personal property was $150,000. It is not uncommon for an insurance company, using heavy-handed deprecation, to value your personal property at 50 percent or less of its current replacement-cost value. In this instance, you would be left with $75,000 to replace $150,000 worth of property. This places a very heavy burden upon you, the property owner, to try to repurchase all of this property, submit replacement receipts for the depreciation holdback, and wait for the check so that you can go buy more items and submit more receipts—and on and on, until you just get tired and give up.

The fact is that no one will repurchase all of his or her destroyed items, which is exactly why the insurance industry set up the game in this manner.

---

[25]   *Property Loss Adjusting* by James Markham

Again, they sell you the illusion of replacement-cost coverage, but they then erect barriers to assure that you never actually receive the full benefits of the policy.

Turning our attention to the application of depreciation on real property, i.e., your home or commercial building, insurance companies follow the same patterns in their application of depreciation to building items. We recently had an insurance company take 30 percent depreciation on the plumbing system of a five-year-old home that was a total loss from a fire. Using this depreciation schedule, my client's plumbing, according to the insurance company, would have only had a twenty-year useful life expectancy.

On this same claim, they took 28 percent depreciation on their windows, 35 percent on their wood-burning stove, and 23 percent on the heating and air-conditioning ductwork. By the time they got finished, they had taken an 18 percent overall depreciation of this five-year-old structure. To suggest that a home's useful life expectancy is only thirty years is ridiculous. We know of many homes from our home neighborhood that were built in about 1955 and are in as good condition today as they were then, and they have never had to replace their plumbing or the heating ductwork.

The application of excessive depreciation is rampant. The most common and heavily depreciated items are floor coverings and paint. These items do actually depreciate faster than other building components, but rarely at the rates that we commonly see used by the insurance companies. Most adjusters do not inquire as to when you last painted your house and often use arbitrary values that have no relationship to the actual condition of the paint at the time of loss.

Another trick that is commonly used by insurance company adjusters is to depreciate repair items. The rules that guide the practice of insurance adjusters dictate that repairs are not subject to depreciation, because you are not replacing the item, only fixing it. The adjuster-training textbooks suggest that when trying to explain depreciation to a consumer, the adjuster should explain it in terms of betterment. For instance, if you have a ten-year-old roof with a life expectancy of twenty years and it gets destroyed in a windstorm, the fair value of the roof at the time of loss was 50 percent of the current replacement value, based upon its age at the time of loss. The consumer is made better by the fact that she got a new roof for an older roof, and when the ten-year-old roof would have worn out, she has now gained ten more years of useful life on the replacement roof.

What we commonly see in practice is insurance companies taking depreciation on the repair of a roof. Let's say that the insurer agrees to replace one slope of the roof. All too often, we find them taking depreciation on this partial replacement, which is actually a repair, not a replacement at all.

Another common trick is taking depreciation on partial repairs of framing. Assume your home had a fire that burned six of the thirty roof trusses that make up your roof system. Many insurers put replacement of the roof trusses in their evaluations and then apply depreciation to the replacement trusses. Thinking back to the term *betterment*, will the consumer be made better if six of his thirty trusses are new? When the rest of the house falls down from decay in 200 years, will these six trusses still be standing? Under the concept of betterment, the consumer has received no betterment by the replacement of these six roof trusses.

The list goes on and on. We see drywall repairs from water damage, where the insurer agrees to cut out the bottom two feet of drywall around the room that was water damaged, and then they apply depreciation to the new drywall repairs. We often see exterior siding repairs depreciated in a similar manner.

One explanation for the insurance adjuster's misunderstanding of the proper application of depreciation is that most insurance companies have switched to a practice of using relatively abbreviated training programs. It is not uncommon for a major insurance company to have a two-, three-, or four-week adjuster-training program. You simply cannot train an insurance adjuster to any reasonable level of competence in two to four weeks.

Another reason for the misapplication of depreciation is the lack of training added to the computer software program's terminology. When using Xactimate, if you were to estimate the water damages repair mentioned above, you would enter into the computer system "Replace." Then, if you are replacing the drywall perimeter of the room up to the two-foot height, the system would calculate the number of square feet and enter this number into the damage evaluation. While the system says that you are replacing, let's say, ninety square feet of drywall, this is not an actual replacement of drywall, which is a depreciable event.

The fact is that a partial replacement of a building component is considered a repair and not a replacement by the insurance industry. It has been this way for decades, at least, until recently. Partial repairs are not subject to depreciation—period. If you find your insurance company applying excessive depreciation or depreciating partial repairs, call the company out on it. Fight back because the facts are in your favor. Ask them to provide a written explanation for their application of depreciation to your loss, and do not allow them to depreciate a repair. Think logically, and put your arguments in writing. If they apply 35 percent depreciation to paint a room you had repainted just a year ago, put it to them in writing, and make them revise their position or justify it. A quick Internet search will help you find many good articles to support this position.

CHAPTER EIGHT

What if the Expert Is wrong?

We recently had a claim on a commercial cabinet shop that was burned in the middle of the night by an arsonist. The evidence revealed that there were twenty-six different points of origin, meaning that there were twenty-six fires set within the building. The owners, Chuck and Therese, had played by the rules, and they spent a decade building their business into one of the premier custom-cabinet shops in the Southwest. Their work was highly acclaimed, and they had received numerous awards for excellence in their craftsmanship and for their business success.

But the insurance company's adjuster, upon finding that the fires were intentionally set and knowing the economic troubles that resulted from the 2008 recession, immediately decided that Chuck and Therese must have set this fire themselves, probably because their business was not doing well. The insurance company then retained a CPA/expert to comb through every personal and business financial record he could find, in an attempt to find some financial problems that they could use to show that Chuck and Therese were motivated to intentionally burn down their own business.

After months of highly invasive inquiries into their lives, the insurance company's CPA/expert, being truly unable to find a real financial motive, authored a report suggesting that they might have burned their building down because they could rent a similar-size building for much less than their current mortgage payment. Even a motivated insurance company could not buy into this absurd theory and it finally began issuing small claim payments.

The fact is, Chuck and Therese were very responsible businesspeople who did not owe on anything other than their commercial building and their home mortgages. They had a nice savings account, and their business, even though it had slowed slightly during the recession, was poised to have a banner year with the recession in the rearview mirror and more than a million dollars in new orders under contract for the coming year. Throughout the insurance company's investigation, its representatives all ignored Chuck and Therese's belief that the fire was set by a recently fired employee. The insurance company had decided Chuck and Therese were guilty and all of its efforts were focused on proving that, so as to avoid payment of their claim.

Unfortunately, by the time the insurance company's investigation was completed and nominal payments finally were issued, it was too late to save their business. All of their twenty-seven employees had taken other jobs because they could not go without paychecks for the four months that the investigation took to complete. And because the insurance company refused to provide any financial assistance until its investigation was complete, Chuck and Therese had no money to set up a temporary shop to remake products for their pending orders. Hence, they lost existing orders, and no one was interested in a bid on a new job from a shop that was currently out of business, thereby causing further economic losses.

But to add insult to injury, the CPA/expert retained by the insurance company had the audacity to take Chuck and Therese's actual accountant-prepared profit and loss (P&L) statements and revise their actual earnings downward in a blatant attempt to undervalue their loss of business income. In litigation, our financial expert said that he had never seen a CPA revise actual P&L statements of a business in this manner, and he was deeply critical of the suggestion by the insurance company's CPA that his modified P&L statements reflected the actual earnings of the business. Of course, using these artificially depressed numbers as the basis for projecting future revenues caused a huge reduction in the insurance company's calculation of lost business income.

In the end, these issues of bias and wrongdoing were exposed, and a significant seven-figure settlement was agreed upon. But even a large settlement like this could not restore Chuck and Therese's reputation or their financial position before the fire loss. The insurance company had abandoned them in their darkest hour, using its experts against them in an attempt to save money on payment of their claim.

Changes in the way insurance companies handle claims over the last decade has spawned an exponential growth in the expert/consultant industry. Traditionally, an expert was a master craftsman, an engineer, an architect, a doctor, or an accountant. Such experts were often practicing professionals in their fields who could be called upon to provide expertise on questions within their field of knowledge and training. But today, an entire industry of experts has evolved from working professionals to firms designed primarily to provide insurance companies with expert opinions on a variety of claims issues, from the causation of damages to the method of repairs to the value of the claim. Engineers, roofing consultants, accountants, and others provide their "expert" opinions on many questions of fact that arise in the processing of insurance claims.

For instance, your roof might have been damaged by a violent hailstorm, causing you to make a claim to your insurance company. Your insurance company responds by sending an adjuster to inspect the damages. If the claims process works as it was initially designed, the adjuster confirms the damages, prepares a loss evaluation, and issues payment for your claim. Sadly, there are very few insurance companies today who still process claims in this manner.

Most insurance companies have removed all discretion from the front-line adjuster, and instead, the claims manager now micromanages the claim from a desk thousands of miles away. Often, the adjuster will tell us that he has been instructed to have the damages inspected by an "expert." Most often, the adjuster does not choose the expert; rather, it is the insurance company that chooses the expert that will be conducting inspections on its behalf. None of what we have discussed is unreasonable or improper, provided that the expert is truly an expert in the field required and that he or she is fair, honest, and unbiased in all determinations.

Unfortunately, all too often lately, the insurance companies choose an "expert" or "consultant" who has little or no real training in the field of knowledge required and who is not operating as an unbiased expert, giving a factual report to the insurance company on the issues being investigated. We routinely find architects or civil engineers investigating damages that are beyond the scope of their training and expertise. Many operate under the umbrella of large, national engineering firms that provide credibility for their opinions. You see, in the engineering world, it is considered proper for any engineer or architect in the firm to conduct field investigations, and they can then produce an engineering report that is signed and stamped by an engineer in the firm who is licensed in the state where the claim arises.

In a recent large commercial claim, an architect was brought in before our involvement, and he wrote a report saying there was no hail damage to the roofs. These types of reports are all too common. Indeed, following the 2010 hailstorm in Phoenix, we saw literally dozens of these types of reports that suggested there were no hail damages; yet, we recovered payment for damages on virtually all of these claims.

In this particular case, the consumer was referred to our firm. We notified the insurance company that we intended to conduct an inspection with an engineer, and we invited the company to participate. The insurer responded with a civil engineer for the same engineering firm, and we took the time to research that person prior to our scheduled meeting. At our meeting, we informed her that we had checked her background and the civil-engineering curriculum from the university where she obtained her degree, and we found no coursework or other training on roofing systems that would qualify her as an expert on hail damages to roofing materials. She admitted that she had no formal training other than her on-the-job experience; yet, this was the person the insurance company was relying upon to decide if there were covered damages to the policyholder's roofs.

She attended the site inspection, telling us that she was only asked to observe our engineer's investigation. Despite multiple offers, she refused to actively engage in a joint investigation with our engineers. Our engineer would ask her technical questions to determine her level of competence, which she would refuse to answer. These questions caused her to spend much of her time walking around the rooftops and taking an occasional picture while we were doing our investigation. To our surprise, three weeks after this site meeting, we received a thirty-eight-page engineering report authored by her that mimicked the architect's previous report and concluded that there were no hail damages to these roofs. This matter was recently resolved when a panel of three independent appraisers awarded the policyholder more than a million and a half dollars for his damages.

This situation raises the question: How is it that three independent damage appraisers were able to confirm hail damages to these roofs, when two insurance-company experts, an engineer and an architect, found there to be no damage? The answer is both simple and disturbing. Many insurance companies are using experts with only a slight degree of familiarity in the subject matter, and they are often engaging biased experts who are willing to "sell" favorable opinions of fact to insurance companies.

As discussed earlier in this book, a tremendous amount of pressure has been exerted on claims departments to hold down the costs of claims. Remember, the less the insurance company pays out in claims, the more profit is retained for the company. The temptation is simply too great for some insurance companies to not engage in these deceptive practices. And, because it is so difficult to prove intentional wrongdoing, there is little to lose and much to gain from such a program.

Due to the substantial amounts of money involved in providing expert services to insurance companies, there is no shortage of "experts" willing to participate in this process. After all, if an insurance company can save more than a million dollars, as they tried to do on the claim referenced above, it is worth spending a few thousand dollars on an expert report.

The obvious question you are probably asking is, *Are you saying that there are insurance companies that are telling their experts to mislead the public in their reports?* Generally, the answer is *no!* These experts understand the process without instruction. They know the answers the insurance company is looking for, and because the insurance company is their customer (often a very important customer), they want to satisfy their customer's needs. In these situations, their needs, often, are not the truth, but rather a predetermined conclusion that will save the insurance company substantial money in claims payments. The insurance companies do not need to micromanage these experts; rather, they can achieve the same result by simply removing unwilling or uncooperative "experts" from their approved vendor list.

It may come as a surprise to most insurance consumers, but this corrupt process of insurance companies using biased experts has been well documented. Just such a practice was at the center of a class-action lawsuit in Oklahoma in 2006 that resulted in a $13 million dollar verdict for the plaintiffs. [26] This lawsuit alleged that a major insurance company hired a Texas-based engineering firm that intentionally undervalued damage to homes and/or claimed that the damage was caused by other factors, such as faulty construction, rather than tornado damage. According to a CNN report, "The jury ruled that [the insurance company] 'recklessly disregarded' its duty to deal fairly and act in good faith with the [insureds] and that it 'intentionally and with malice' breached its duties as the couple's insurance company. The jury further found 'clear and convincing evidence' that [the insurance company] recklessly disregarded its duty to act fairly and in good faith with members of the class action by employing [the engineering firm] and its independent adjusters."[27]

The same engineering firm was also involved in a 2006 investigation by the attorney general of the state of Mississippi over its alleged wrongdoing in preparing damage reports for the same insurance company on hundreds of homeowners' claims resulting from Hurricane Katrina.[28] In this incident, two sisters who supervised claims handlers for the insurer served as whistleblowers to expose how the insurance company's adjusters manipulated engineering reports to change the cause of damage from wind (a covered cause of loss) to storm surge (not covered by the insurance company's policy) so as to deny coverage for legitimate claims.

This same engineering firm was at the center of another case where it was alleged that the insurance company knowingly used a biased consulting

---

[26]   *Insurance Journal* May 30, 2006

[27]   http://www.cnn.com/2006/US/05/26/statefarm.verdict/

[28]   The Washington Post Sisters Blew Whistle on Katrina Claims By MICHAEL KUNZELMAN The Associated Press Saturday, August 26, 2006; 8:36 PM

report to deny coverage. For that case, the Texas Supreme Court, in this case, sided with a consumer in a dispute over damages caused to the foundation of his home from a water leak. [29]

This problem is not restricted to just this one engineering firm; that firm, being one of the biggest, has just been caught more than the others. Also, these are only the cases where there was the will and determination on the part of the insured to hold the insurance company accountable for wrongdoing. We are confident that many more similar acts go undetected or unprosecuted due to the time and cost required to hold an insurance company accountable.

This increased use of biased experts provides insurance companies with a mechanism for issuing denials of legitimate claims, and it has the added benefit of reducing their exposure to bad-faith damages. As we discussed in an earlier chapter, bad faith arises when an insurance company intentionally or recklessly delays or denies a claim when its liability is reasonably clear. Thus, when insurance companies retain consultants who prepare biased reports, this gives the insurance company a factual basis for denying the claim. Put another way, the use of such a third-party expert provides the insurance company with a "scapegoat" or an excuse if the claim results in litigation. The insurance company's first defense will be that the damages are as depicted in the engineer's report. The second defense will be to argue that the company simply relied upon the findings of an independent expert, and even if those findings were in error, it could not possibly have acted in bad faith!

Under the law, if there is no clear evidence of improper conduct, a dispute over coverage on a claim is said to be "fairly debatable." What this means is that while the insurance company's conclusion may be wrong, the denial of coverage or another claims-handling decision does not rise to the level of bad-faith conduct. It can be difficult to prove that a consultant did not use reasonable care and generally accepted procedures to investigate the facts before issuing an opinion, and it may be even harder to prove that the insurance company had prior knowledge of this.

---

[29]   State Farm Lloyds v. Nicolau, 951 S.W.2d 444 (Tex. 1997)

But in cases such as those referenced above, where there are catastrophic damages to a region, it is easier to compare multiple expert reports to establish a pattern. Unfortunately, most consumers do not have the benefit of having multiple reports on similar damages from a single firm to rely on. In these cases, the claims are often wrongfully denied, and consumers are left holding the bag and paying for losses themselves—losses that they bought insurance to cover.

In our business, we see this every day, and it has become an epidemic in the insurance-claim business. In days past, it was only occasionally that we would have a biased expert on a claim file, but today, it is more the rule than the exception. This is not to say that all experts are bad, because nothing could be further from the truth. In fact, we would say that many honestly try to provide a fair and competent opinion on the loss. Regrettably, though, there is an increasing number of such "experts" who will say whatever it takes to make their insurance-company customers happy.

The fact is that some experts lie, and many of them start their lies with their resumes or curriculum vitaes (CVs). We routinely find that the CVs of experts exaggerate their training and expertise. We once had an expert present himself as an engineer; however, after an exhaustive investigation, we confirmed that he did not have an engineering degree and he was not qualified to render an opinion on our client's damages. Our qualified engineer's opinion held the day, after this misrepresentation was exposed.

Another recent story involved water damage from a broken water heater in a multimillion-dollar home of one our clients. The water heater failed, which caused eighty gallons of hot water to leak into the home. This water caused extensive damages, including damage to the ceramic tile flooring, which is common in water-loss claims. Floor tile is installed with a water-based mastic that adheres the tile to the concrete slab. Often, when the floors become saturated by water, the mastic loses its adherence. The loss of adherence is real damage, as the loose tiles will be subject to increased risk of breakage. It is relatively easy to identify this type of damage by the hollow sound the tile makes when it is tapped with a firm object.

In that case, the insurance company, in an attempt to avoid paying for the replacement of the tile floors, brought in a tile "expert." His CV and his business card alleged that he was from a "ceramic tile institute," which we had never heard of, but it sounded impressive. After some investigation, we made a call to this "institute," where we were told by the person who answered the phone that their main office was not in California, where they listed their office, but in Phoenix, Arizona. We then had an associate call the Phoenix number, where he was told that the main office was in California and that they were just a branch office.

As it turned out, these two former tile installers had decided that it was easier to sell their services to insurance companies as tile "experts" rather than doing the backbreaking work of actually installing tile. The whole point of their services seemed to be to write expert reports saying that the tile was not damaged by water, but rather, that any damage was due to defective installation. And this was all being done by alleging they were credentialed experts through this fictitious "institute."

Not all experts are employed by insurance companies. Not long ago, we had a claim where the experts were fire investigators for the local fire department. In this loss, the fire investigators made an immediate decision that this fire was intentionally set and they then engaged in an investigation designed not to find the truth, but to prove their theory. Their approach was eventually proven to not be credible. But, before the truth came out, as a result of this inept fire investigation, our client was arrested for felony arson and placed in jail. When the flawed investigation was finally exposed, the charges were eventually dropped by the county prosecutor's office "in the interest of justice." Regrettably, the insurance company's fire investigators were encouraged to withhold evidence from the prosecutor in an attempt to obtain a conviction and to deny coverage for this claim.

It took the retention of real experts, years of litigation, and massive costs to prove this customer's innocence in causing the loss. This case eventually received national notoriety through a series of stories on ABC's *Nightline* news program. Imagine having to endure years of "litigation hell" to prove your innocence after a fire rips through your home. And imagine that your insurance company is deliberately working against you, subjecting you to the possibility of twenty-seven years in prison for a crime you did not commit, simply to save money on the payment of your claim.

It is a fact that expert reports are not always right. Do not be tricked into thinking that just because your insurance company hired an engineer who wrote a report that identifies another cause of your damages that this opinion is necessarily correct. And just because the "expert" has engineering credentials, this does not mean that he or she is a fair and honest vendor. We have handled dozens of claims where an engineer had authored a report before we were hired that stated there was no damage, and yet more than 98 percent of those cases ended with our recovery of damages for those clients. In fact, we recently completed a claim on a large apartment complex in Dallas, where the insurer had denied the claim based on an engineer's report stating that there was no hail damage. We settled this claim without litigation for $1.6 million.

The best way you can protect yourself is to ask a lot of questions. Do not allow someone to enter your property without a business card. If your adjuster says he is bringing in an expert, demand that he provide you with the expert's name and CV prior to the visit. You have a right, under the rules of good faith, to know just what credentials the expert has, particularly when that person's expertise is being relied upon by your insurance company to determine the outcome of your claim.

CHAPTER NINE

Common Estimating Errors and Deceptions

The part of your claim that deals with estimating the costs to repair your home or your commercial building is by far the most difficult part of claims handling to pin down to a specific wrongful practice. Because of the nature of construction estimating, the number of ways that you can be deceived is only limited by the callous intentions of the devious mind. If you do not have extensive knowledge of construction practices and are not familiar with the restoration estimating software that is used to determine the fair-value cost to restore your real property to its pre-loss condition, your chance of obtaining a full fair-value claim settlement is highly unlikely. We will attempt here to address some of these improper estimating practices and the more common omissions, but be aware that there are as many ways to cheat as there are cheaters.

One of the more common omissions that we see is the failure to clean surfaces before painting. Whenever a surface is designated to be repainted, the proper method for repainting is to apply the new paint to a clean surface. Manufacturers spell this out on the labels of most paint products because their products require a clean surface in order for them to adequately cover and adhere to the surface being painted. If your insurer is repainting your walls and ceiling, be sure that cleaning is included in the loss evaluation, or you are being short-changed. This is also true for exterior painting. In fact, exteriors are even more exposed to dust and dirt than interiors. These surfaces must also be cleaned before painting them. This same process is required before the application of the smoke-sealer coating to smoke exposed framing as well.

Another important area of the loss evaluation to double check is the room and building dimensions. While the Xactimate program now requires the estimator to sketch the entire building before entering the scope of repair items, there are other versions of this program that do not require the sketch process. In "sketch," if the drawing is accurate, the program will automatically calculate the correct square footages for each scope item. That being said, we still commonly see mistakes with the area-dimension entries.

After verification of the dimensions entries, the next step is to review the quantities being allowed in the insurer's loss evaluation. There are too many ways to make a mistake to cover in this book, but some of the most common mistakes include roof restorations. This is because some roof operations are entered by the square foot, while others are entered by the square (a square is a ten-foot by ten-foot area, equal to one hundred square feet). Verify that the size of your roof matches the quantities spelled out in their loss evaluation.

Also, another item to double check in the estimate is depreciation. As discussed in Chapter 7, insurers commonly depreciate partial repairs. Just because the program nomenclature says "replace drywall," this does not mean that this is considered a replacement under an insurance policy. If you are only replacing the bottom two feet of drywall in a room, this is a repair, and no depreciation should be applied to this operation. This same procedure holds true for partial roof repairs and for painting of one wall (assuming it can be matched).

Another common practice by insurers is to use the wrong grade (quality) for items such as carpeting, cabinets, and lighting fixtures. What Xactimate calls "high-grade" in its program is, in reality, more of a nice "builder's grade" product. Ask your adjuster for the printout from Xactimate that provides the operation's description. This description spells out the type of quality for this line item in the program.

Assuming you have the correct cabinet grade, the next step is to confirm that your adjuster has included all of the extras that are common to kitchen cabinetry. If your cabinets had handles, this is an add-on item in Xactimate.

Did you have glass doors on some of your upper cabinets? This is also an add-on. How about soft-close drawers, trash bins, crown moldings? These must all be added on separately, as these are not included in the cabinetry provided by the program. If your cabinetry makes a ninety-degree turn, be sure that your adjuster has included the extra charges for this miter cut in his countertop replacement.

If you have suffered a fire loss, be certain that any framing that may have been exposed to smoke and soot is cleaned and sealed properly. We have been in homes that had a fire years earlier and when you walk in the door, you can still smell the odor of fire, even after the home has been restored. This is likely because their insurer and/or their contractor left them with smoke and soot residue in wall cavities and in attic areas.

A new trend in the insurance industry is to take out the cost of many of the items contained in the loss evaluation's "general conditions" area and denote them as payable "as incurred." Items such as building permits, engineering costs, architectural costs, temporary toilets, temporary power, temporary fencing, caution tape, and commercial or residential supervision are among the more common items that are not included in the insurance company's ACV claim payments.

Just as with contractor's overhead and profit, these scope items are all a part of the actual cash value of the loss. The policy promises to pay you for the actual cash value of loss up front, and if you have a replacement-cost policy, you can recover the additional holdback monies when repairs are completed. The key to the deceptive nature of this wrongful withholding of your money is based in the policy's promise to pay you the actual cash value of your loss. As with the contractor's overhead and profit, when your home was built, the cost of the home included amounts for building permits, job supervision, architectural plans, engineering plans, a portable toilet for the workers, etc. Therefore, when a loss occurs, a portion of the actual cash-value loss would necessarily include these costs.

There is no policy requirement we have ever seen that requires these costs to be incurred before your insurer owes you payment for them. In fact, under most standard policies, the only losses that must be incurred before they are payable are the depreciation holdback on a replacement-cost policy, law and ordinance costs, and additional living expenses (ALE) (residential) and loss of business income/extra expenses (commercial). These loss expenses are paid on an "as incurred" basis. Other than the aforementioned items, your insurer owes you the actual cash value of all other expenses required to restore your property.

You might ask: If they are required to pay these items, why do they not pay them? The answer is simple: it saves them a lot of money. So, they make up their own rules. You see, the insurance company can say that it does not pay this cost or that cost until it is incurred, but the courts will surely say differently. Unfortunately, most consumers do not want to take these matters to litigation, so the insurance industry gets away with reducing their claim payments through this improper practice.

Also, because most people do not understand their rights under an insurance policy, they do not understand that the insurance company is liable for these payments up front in their actual cash-value payment. And like with the past trend to deliberately withhold contractor's overhead and profit, because of the court's ruling in *Campbell*, they can no longer be punished adequately to completely deter this type of wrongful conduct.

If you see the words *as incurred* on your loss evaluation, demand a written explanation for this position and ask that they cite to the policy language that they have relied upon to withhold these monies. Also, speak to an attorney or a public adjuster if need be. This is an improper withholding of your money, and these types of wrongful practices must be eliminated from the claims-adjusting business. Unless consumers hold insurance companies accountable for the written promises that they made when they sold you their policy, this practice is likely to continue. If they don't want to pay these costs in their actual cash-value claim payments, they have the power to rewrite their policies to exclude these costs, rather than misinterpreting this coverage.

CHAPTER TEN

Coinsurance Deceptions and Improper Applications of Deductibles

Coinsurance requirements are common in insurance policies, yet few people outside of the insurance business know what they are and how they work. Coinsurance is the joint assumption of risk by two or more parties. In a typical property-insurance policy, it is usually the risk assumed by the insurance company and that assumed by the consumer. The purpose of this policy provision is to encourage consumers to accurately report the values of property so that they do not underinsure their property. You might ask: Why would anyone deliberately underinsure his or her property? The answer is simple. The vast majority of losses are only partial losses, so the chance of needing coverage for the full value of the property is rare. So thrifty and insurance savvy consumers can save money in the form of the premiums paid for their policies by insuring their properties for less than their full value.

In order to deter this type of underinsurance, many policies have a coinsurance requirement. The most common coinsurance requirement is 80 percent, which means that the consumer must insure his property for at least 80 percent of its full replacement-cost value. If a loss occurs and the insurance company discovers that the coinsurance requirement has not been met, it can assess a coinsurance penalty against the consumer to recover a portion of the loss. This forces the policyholder to participate in the loss up to the required percentage.

To better explain this, let's use an example. Bob has a commercial building with a current replacement value of $150,000 that he has insured for $100,000. The policy he purchased has an 80 percent coinsurance requirement. Bob has a fire loss that does $50,000 in damage to his building. The insurance adjuster does a calculation of the replacement cost of his building as it was at the time of loss and determines that the replacement cost of his building was $150,000. Assuming that he had a $500 policy deductible, Bob's claim payable would be calculated as follows:

Loss payable =

Coverage purchased   x   Loss   -   Deductible
(Property value x coinsurance)

Hence, Bob's claim would be paid as follows:

$100,000   or $100,000   = .8333 x $50,000
($150,000*80%) $120,000

= $41,665 - $500 = $41,165 claim payable

Consequently, Bob must participate in this loss not only with his deductible; because he underinsured his property, he will also only receive a prorated portion of his loss. This decision cost Bob an additional $8,335 plus his deductible. Had Bob insured his property properly, his only cost would have been the policy deductible.

But what if Bob did not really underinsure his property? What if the methods used by his adjuster do not accurately calculate the real replacement cost of his building?

Other questions also arise from this, such as: What is Bob's expertise in determining the value of his building? Did Bob rely upon his agent to set the policy limits? What is his agent's responsibility for setting the policy limits of coverage? And what responsibility does the insurance company's policy underwriter have in this determination of the appropriate levels of coverage Bob needs to fully insure his building? Did the insurance company or the agent ever inform Bob that he was underinsuring his building before the loss?

This is a complex issue that requires a great deal of skill and investigation into how the policy coverage limits were set and the party responsible for this determination. Also, the laws vary from state to state on whether or not an agent can be held liable for an error in the placement of coverage.

So why bring this issue up here? The reason is that we are seeing a sigificant increase in the number of claims that are being scrutinized by insurers for meeting the policy's coinsurance requirements, and we are also seeing egregious miscalculations of what is to be included in the insurance company's calculation of the replacement-cost valuation. Suffice it to say that it is easy for an adjuster to exaggerate the full replacement cost of a building if he is so motivated. And we believe that the insurance company's underwriter has some responsibility to the policyholder to inform him if he is selecting a policy limit that does not meet the coinsurance requirements. We often refer to this belated application of coinsurance to a loss as "post-loss underwriting."

It is easy to see how an insurer could be motivated to exaggerate the coinsurance penalty so as to save money in claims payments. And as you remember from the first couple of chapters, every dollar saved in claim payments is another dollar of net income for the insurance company.

Another very common improper claims practice is in regards to the application of the policy deductible. This issue has been the subject of several articles over the years; yet, we continue to see the same improper applications of policy deductibles time after time. The issue is with the absorption of the deductible by the excess losses.

We are taught in our formal insurance-industry training to first apply the policy deductible to the total loss and then to apply any limitations of coverage as set forth in the policy. However, we often see adjusters applying the policy deductible to the loss-payable portion of the claim rather than to the total loss. This difference can be best explained through an example.

Let's assume that Rick has a homeowner's policy that includes coverage for theft and has a policy deductible of one hundred dollars. While Rick is on vacation, a burglar breaks into Rick's home and steals his TV, which has a replacement value of $500; his camera, valued at $400; and $350 in cash that he had in his nightstand. Rick's policy is a standard ISO form HO-3, which has a limitation of coverage for cash of $200.

Rick's claim from this theft event should be determined as follows:

TV	$500
Camera	$400
Cash	$350
Total Loss	$1,250
Excess cash loss	($150)
Claim Payable	$1,100

Deductible of $100 absorbed within the excess cash loss

We often see insurance adjusters determining Rick's loss payable as follows:

TV	$500
Camera	$400
Cash	$350
Total Loss	$1,250
Excess cash loss	($150)
Claim Payable	$1,100
Deductible	($100)
The Wrong Claim Payable	$1,000

Rick's adjuster would not be allowed to apply the one-hundred-dollar policy deductible to the loss payable because the special limit of coverage for theft of cash left Rick with an uncovered loss of $150. As such, Rick has already participated in the loss through his excess cash loss.

This example is deliberately simplified to help you to understand the concept. Now imagine that you have a commercial building with a $500,000 policy deductible and you have a million dollars in mold damages from a water intrusion, where mold coverage is limited to $10,000 under the policy.

Absorption of the policy deductible can have a huge impact on your ultimate recovery from this loss.

We often see adjusters fail to properly absorb a policy deductible as they should, without us first bringing it to their attention. In fact, we know of insurance companies that deliberately instruct their adjusters to not properly apply policy deductibles to claims, as we observed firsthand after Hurricane Floyd ripped across the northeast in 1999.

The wrongful practice in applying deductibles was also common following the Northridge earthquake and these practices led to expensive litigation for some insurers that were misapplying the policy deductibles for earthquake losses. Certain insurers got sued because they calculated the 10 percent earthquake deductible on the total amount of coverage written, rather than as 10 percent of the amount of the claim.

One such instance involved a large HOA that had an $85 million policy, where the insurance company was applying an $8.5 million deductible to their $10.5 million loss. When the HOA board asked if we could help them, my partner and I just looked at each other and smiled and assured them that we could indeed help.

There is no reason that a consumer should have to retain help to obtain the benefits that he or she paid for under an insurance policy, yet, day after day, the need for professional representation becomes ever more apparent. The claims game is rigged, and it more often than not requires someone who knows the rules and knows how to play the game as well as or better than the insurance company.

CHAPTER ELEVEN

Matching and Cosmetic Losses

One of the most important claim issues, and the one that has a significant impact on homeowners, is the issue of "matching." What happens when your lower kitchen cabinets are damaged by a water-line break, but replacement cabinets to match the upper cabinets are no longer available? What if the roof is damaged by a windstorm and matching roof shingles are no longer available? What is the insurance company's responsibility under the policy?

The answer to this question lies more on where you live than with what the policy says. This is an issue that has been litigated many times, and because the matter involves insurance, which must be litigated on a state-by-state basis, the answer to this question is different depending upon which court makes the ruling. Some courts vigorously adhere to the basic principles of indemnity, holding that repair of damages must result in an aesthetically pleasing result. Or, in laymen's terms, the repairs must match the existing building components in materials, colors, and finishes.

Other courts have been more restrictive in their interpretation of the policy's promise of coverage, ruling that the policy is only intended to replace the portions of the building that actually suffered damages from a covered peril. This reasoning ignores the traditional application of coverage by insurance companies, and it mistakenly buys in to the insurance companies' misreading of their own policies. In these cases, the courts have ruled that the insurance policy does not require the insurer to replace areas that were not damaged. Regrettably, this leaves consumers with either a mismatched area of their building or a huge out-of-pocket cost to make an aesthetically proper repair.

In the mid-1990s, when this issue first surfaced, we wrote to the well-respected insurance treatise, *FC&S Bulletins*, which is a subsidiary of the Insurance Services Office, who is the author of the ISO insurance policies used by many insurance companies. The *FC&S Bulletins* is a publication that discusses how the language of the policies that the ISO writes is intended to be interpreted. An additional feature of the *FC&S Bulletins* is a question and answer (Q&A) section that is published periodically, where claims adjusters can write in and present a specific set of facts on one of their claims, and the editors of the *FC&S Bulletins* provide a detailed explanation of how they believe the policy language should respond to these situations. It is very informative and interesting to read some of the questions and answers in this publication.

One such question, which we presented, asked about the new positions (at that time) being taken by insurance companies, stating that their policies do not owe to match. The editors of the *FC&S* provided a well-reasoned answer to this question. At that time, insurance companies were taking the position that if the upper cabinets were not damaged, they did not owe to replace them, even though the new lower cabinets would not match the existing upper cabinets. Similar arguments were being made as to matching many other building components, such as roof shingles or exterior siding.

The insurance companies devised a creative argument in an attempt to restrict coverage by arguing that the policy states that they will repair or replace "that part of the building" that is damaged. In their view, "that part of a building" meant each individual shingle or individual piece of siding, rather than the more logical interpretation that "a shingle may be part of a building but is, more properly, a part of a roof." Similarly, a strip of siding is a part of a wall. And it is the walls and the roof that become "parts" of the building.

The editors of the *FC&S Bulletins* shocked the insurance world with their resounding affirmation that yes, indeed, the insurance policy does in fact owe the insured for a matching repair. They supported their opinion citing the basic tenets of insurance, the "principle of indemnity" and the insured's "reasonable expectations." They said, "The insured is told that he will be made whole and restored to a pre-loss condition; based on this promise, he reasonably expects this will be done in the event of a loss. He expects to be fully indemnified."[30]

It has been many years since this *FC&S* editor's opinion was first issued. Since this time, the *FC&S Bulletins* has hedged their position somewhat, acknowledging that the issue of matching has been adjudicated in courtrooms across the country with somewhat different results. However, even today, the editors in the online version of *FC&S Bulletins* maintain that, in their opinion, the insurance policy should owe for matching repairs.[31]

The results of the various court decisions give us different rules for different jurisdictions. So the question of whether your insurance policy covers matching repairs may be more a function of where you live than what your policy says.

While the majority have found that the insurance company owes for matching repairs in the event of a covered loss, there have been some decisions that confound the logical mind. One such case is that of the 2008 Texas Court of Appeals ruling in the *All Saints Catholic Church* matter.[32] In this ridiculous ruling, the court took the position that the insurance company only owed for the cost of replacing the individual roof tiles that suffered hail damage, even though these roof tiles were no longer available for purchase and in spite of the fact presented at trial that removing the damaged tiles would cause damage many more additional tiles. In its ruling, the court ignored the fact that replacement tiles could not be installed without damaging the existing tiles, and it ignored the fact that the new tiles would not match the existing tiles. According to this court, it was acceptable that the church, after suffering a covered loss, would have to pay out of pocket for a substantial portion of the repairs to its roof, even though it had a properly functioning and matching roof prior to this hailstorm.

---

[30] Letter from FC&S on File

[31] http://www.nationalunderwriterpc.com/Pages/default.aspx

[32] All Saints Catholic Church v. United National Insurance Company, 257 S.W.3d 800

Notwithstanding this court decision, in a very recent litigation regarding the issue of matching, the Minnesota Supreme Court in *Cedar Bluff* has weighed in, in favor of coverage for matching repairs to the Cedar Bluff Townhome Condominium Association's exterior siding when it was shown that the existing siding was no longer available and the new siding did not match the existing siding. In its ruling, the court stated that "the plain meaning of the phrase 'comparable material and quality' is material that is *suitable* for matching ... Therefore, in accordance with the plain meaning of the policy language, we construe the phrase 'comparable material and quality' to mean a reasonable color match between new and existing siding when replacing damaged siding."[33]

The court went on to address American Family's argument that the policy did not require it to replace siding that was not damaged. As we discussed above, the insurance company's argument is based upon the idea that the policy only owes to repair the damaged siding. This court analyzed American Family's argument by looking into the policy's promise of coverage for "direct physical loss or damage" and American Family's own definition of the term *physical damage,* meaning "a distinct, demonstrable, and physical alteration."

In this regard, the court rejected the piece-by-piece approach but instead looked at the siding as a whole as they ruled that "Because of the color mismatch resulting from the inability to replace the hail-damaged siding panels with siding of 'comparable material and quality' the covered property—Cedar Bluff's 'buildings'—has sustained a 'distinct, demonstrable, and physical alteration.' Thus, we conclude that the covered property sustained a covered loss."[34]

This court decision and many similar decisions have forced the insurance companies to resort to a new tactic. Rather than taking on the issue of matching directly, they have devised a new tactic.

---

[33] Cedar Bluff Townhome Condo. Ass'n v. American Family Mut. Ins. Co., 857 N.W.2d 290 (2014)

[34] *Cedar Bluff Townhome Condo. Ass'n v. American Family Mut. Ins. Co.,* 857 N.W.2d 290 (2014)

You see, the insurance industry never seems to exhaust its list of tricks to avoid coverage for losses. Their creative use of semantics to make arguments against coverage seems endless.

Remember that about ten years ago, the insurance industry came to the conclusion that it did not have to pay contractor's overhead and profit costs until these costs were incurred, despite the fact that its policies make no mention of the word *incurred* as a requirement of indemnification. As this issue became the subject of multiple lawsuits across the country, insurance companies eventually found it to be unprofitable to continue this practice. Unfortunately, the manner in which insurance is regulated in the United States forces consumers to fight the same battles in each state. So while companies started to pay contractors' overhead and profit costs on claim payments in those jurisdictions where they had lost, they continued to withhold these costs in the states that had not yet ruled on the issue.

The latest trend is in response to the multitude of hail-damage claims, from Texas to Arizona. It is not that there are really that many more hailstorms, but there are more roofing contractors who have discovered that they can make a very good living following these storm events.

The insurance industry seems to be engaged in a concerted effort to encourage its favorite engineers and consultants to include qualifying language in their expert reports to be later used as the basis to deny coverage. The reason we say it's a *concerted* effort is because it seems unlikely that all of a sudden, we would start seeing the same references in reports from different engineering firms and on behalf of different insurance companies, all appearing at or about the same time period, if not for a concerted effort by the insurance industry to steer firms in this direction. Either that or these engineering firms all woke up one day and decided, independently, to insert similar qualifying language into their description of damages in their expert reports. You be the judge.

The most recent trend is for these favorite consultants to identify damages in terms of "functional damages vs. cosmetic damages." Of course, the implication here and the application of this argument is that "cosmetic damages" are not real damage and are not to be afforded coverage under the insurance policy. In looking to the standard language of the ISO form HO-3 policy, the "HO 003 10 00" policy sets forth coverage as follows: "We insure against risk of direct loss to property described in Coverages A and B." The policy then goes into a laundry list of losses that are excluded from coverage under this policy, none of which contain any discussion of either cosmetic or functional damages.

Even more excluded losses can be found in the policy's "exclusions" provision, things like law and ordinance, earth movement, nuclear hazard, and intentional loss—but still nothing at all about cosmetic or functional damages.

In the commercial policy, the ISO form CP 10 30 Causes of Loss – Special Form sets forth coverage as follows:

> A. Covered Causes Of Loss
>
> When Special is shown in the Declarations, Covered Causes of Loss means Risks Of Direct Physical Loss unless the loss is:
>
> 1. Excluded in Section B., Exclusions; or
> 2. Limited in Section C., Limitations; that follow.

Again, there is no reference at all to cosmetic or functional damages, either in the insuring-agreement language or in the exclusions provisions. So, then, where is this coming from? While we are not industry insiders, we suspect that this may be being orchestrated by the insurance industry's Property Loss Research Bureau (PLRB), which is an association of insurance companies dedicated to the advancement of insurance-company coverage issues. Their defense attorneys apparently get together to brainstorm insurance-defense procedures, and it is self-evident that they routinely find inventive ways to bolster insurers' profits through creative new arguments to limit or deny coverage for damages. There can be no other explanation for multiple insurance companies and different engineering firms all mysteriously using the same unique terminology at about the same time. Of course, maybe it is just a coincidence.

The fact remains that no standard-form insurance policy makes a distinction between cosmetic vs. functional damages or sets forth exclusions for such. Yet, over the last four or five years, we have had multiple insurers attempt to make this argument on our clients' claims. In a recent case that we submitted to be resolved through the policy's appraisal provision, our appraiser called us and said that the other appraiser was arguing to the umpire that some of the damages to the property were purely cosmetic and not functional damages. We suggested that at their next meeting, he back into the other appraiser's car fender and then tell him that he is very sorry, but that the damage is only cosmetic and not functional damage. It would be interesting to see his reaction. We have no doubt that he would not be okay with that!

Imagine if your auto insurer was to rely upon such a distinction. There would be millions of cars driving around with dented fenders and bumpers. Some might look like they have been in a demolition derby. If a hailstorm damages your car, is that cosmetic or functional damage? Is it covered? Of course it is cosmetic, and yes, it is covered if you purchased a comprehensive auto-insurance policy. They would have a really hard time selling automobile insurance policies if they attempted to exclude cosmetic damages from coverage, as that is one major motivator to buying auto insurance in the first place: to protect your car from accidental damage.

Having insurance coverage is also required by the bank that loans you the money to buy your car, so that it is protected by insurance in the case of damage. This is likewise the point of purchasing homeowner's insurance protection: to protect your investment in "real" property from damages, be it cosmetic or functional.

Do not allow yourself to be tricked into this insurance trap. This language is deliberately designed to underpay or deny legitimate claims. In most policies, there is no distinction between cosmetic and functional damages. Damage is damage, period—and the policy's promise is for coverage to repair or replace the damaged building component, just the same as it does for your car, and in most states, the promise of coverage includes matching repairs.

Be careful, though, because some insurers are inserting endorsements that limit coverage for the cost of repairs to match or provide new language for functional damages. You must be cognizant of the jurisdiction in which your property is located, as the controlling case law varies significantly from one state to the next, as do the state laws that regulate insurance. To get a definitive answer, start by reviewing the policy coverages and endorsements, check the state insurance statutes, and then find an attorney who knows applicable case law in your jurisdiction.

CHAPTER TWELVE

Emerging Issues and Final Thoughts

The concept of transferring risk in a monetary economy began with the ancient Chinese and Babylonian traders in the third and second millennia BC. The Chinese merchants who traveled treacherous river rapids would redistribute the goods between many vessels to limit the loss due to any one vessel capsizing. Babylonian traders who took a loan to fund their shipments would pay an additional sum to have the loan forgiven if the shipment was stolen or lost at sea. These "insurance practices" continued into the first millennium BC, where the inhabitants of Rhodes created the "general average" which allowed groups of merchants to pay to insure their goods being shipped together. Property Insurance as we know it today has its roots in the Great Fire of London in 1666 which consumed 13,000 homes.[35]

The importance of insurance to a civilized society has been clear for centuries, as was the recognition that spreading the risk among many at a small price could protect the few from certain financial disaster. This was the birth of today's insurance model, which is built upon the statistical concept of the law of large numbers. [36]

Insurance companies are expert in accessing and transferring risks. Actuaries analyze the financial consequences of a risk through mathematics, statistics, and financial theory to predict the likely cost and probability of a

---

[35] Wikipedia (http://en.wikipedia.org/wiki/History_of_insurance)
[36] Wikipedia (http://en.wikipedia.org/wiki/History_of_insurance)

loss event. They have become so proficient that they can predict with near certainty the number of fire losses that any major city will have this year.

Armed with this information, insurance companies can offer insurance products that provide financial security to consumers while assuring a fair profit for the insurance company. In recent years, we have seen several major catastrophic loss events, yet, in the last one hundred years, the property/casualty insurance market has only shown a loss in one year. That is just one year in a hundred! Their modeling is obviously very good in predicting and preparing for loss events.

Insurance companies have also become very good at avoiding the most likely and costly loss events by transferring these risks to government. This transfer of risk has resulted in the National Flood Insurance Program for flood damage. Along our southeastern coastline, we have the Citizens Property Insurance Corporation for hurricane and wind-damage insurance coverage along coastal areas. In California, there is earthquake coverage, via the California Earthquake Authority. While in some instances, insurance companies are required or encouraged to participate in these programs, the major responsibility for the risk of loss for these programs falls upon the federal and/or state government, which means it is your tax dollars that ultimately insures these risks.

Other developments in the transfer of risk are being seen in the middle of the country with respect to inland wind and hail losses. Insurance companies are changing their policies to include large wind and hail deductibles that are separate and distinct from the standard policy deductible. Other changes of late include policy exclusions for cosmetic damages and ACV (actual cash value) roof endorsements, which amend the policy to only pay for the actual cash value of the roof in the event of a covered loss if the roof is more than ten years old, even if you have a replacement-cost policy on the property. In many cases, our clients are surprised to find that these provisions have made their way into their policies, so it is safe to say that in many cases, the consumers are not being adequately notified of these significant changes to their insurance coverage.

Also, we are seeing insurance companies adding provisions that limit coverage for repairs by adding qualifying language to limit their obligation to "common construction and similar materials" rather than "like kind and quality." The ISO has authored a policy-coverage form for insurance companies to amend the coverage provided to functional replacement-cost coverage in their ISO HO 05 30 05 11 and HO 05 31 11 policy forms. These changes in insurance coverage have one common element: they pay less in the event of a covered loss.

Recently, one of America's major insurance companies has begun a practice in preparing their loss evaluations in a manner that we believe will ultimately lead to litigation. The computer estimating software known as Xactimate is offered to its users with more than one price-list database. They offer a "restoration" price list and a "new construction" price list. With the flip of a switch, the adjuster can switch between these price lists—allegedly, to account for the actual conditions of the project being evaluated. The restoration price list is developed to account for the costs of restoring or repairing damages to an existing building. The new-construction price list was developed to estimate the construction costs for building a new building from the ground up. The differences in costs vary by the type of work that is being estimated, but the general rule is that the new-construction price list will yield a significantly lower cost of construction than the restoration price list will.

The reason for this is that when engaging in restoration work, the contractor must work around existing building components. He must protect the existing finishes and fixtures from being damaged as he goes about the restoration work. During construction of a new building, the trades are scheduled to complete their portion of the work in a sequence that makes many of the precautions that a restoration contractor might have to take unnecessary.

For instance, when considering the interior painting of a building, in new construction, the interior painting is most often done before there are any floor coverings, lighting fixtures, and furnishings to protect from overspray paint damages. As such, the painting of a new home or building would be less expensive to complete because the time required to do the work is reduced.

Similarly, when engaging in new construction, the various subcontractors do not have to worry about working around existing landscaping, fences, sidewalks, etc. A roofing contractor can drive a forklift right up to the building to deliver the roof shingles for installation. Driving a forklift up to an existing structure would likely cause damages to lawns, sprinkler systems, shrubbery, etc., making it necessary to either hand-carry the materials onto the roof or pay for damages caused to the landscaping. The new-construction price list takes into consideration the cost savings of building a new building from the ground up, as opposed to completing a restoration of an existing building.

The latest practice by one insurer is to use the new-construction price list on the partial repair (restoration) of a home that has been fire damaged. Despite repeated attempts to correct this wrongful claim practice, this insurer has refused to budge. Their adjuster, whom we have known for years, just shrugs his shoulders and says that this is being dictated by their corporate office and he has no choice except to follow instructions. The net result on one recent claim is an underpayment of nearly $10,000 when compared to the same project evaluated with the restoration price list.

Obviously, underpaying claims in this manner will reduce this insurance company's cost of claims, and as with its wrongful practices of withholding contractor's overhead and profit, the company knows that eventually it will get caught, be sued, and have to pay out some money over this practice. But the money they save in the meantime still makes this sort of conduct profitable. Again, many thanks can go to the United States Supreme Court for its errant wisdom in the *Campbell* ruling.

When insurance companies cannot get what they want through their lobbying efforts of government agencies to change the laws, they just ignore the laws until they are sued enough times that it makes these wrongful practices impractical to continue. Even today, we still find insurance companies failing to pay contractor's overhead and profit on claims.

Judging by all of these changes, one would think that there is some huge problem with insurance companies losing money, yet as we mentioned above, they have only lost money once in the last hundred years. So what is the driving force for all of these changes? The answer is obvious: profits, profits, and more profits. While we all want and need our insurance providers to be profitable for the overall good of society, the increases in revenues generated in the property and casualty insurance market are unprecedented in comparison to any other historical period of time. Insurance companies are no longer satisfied to just make a fair profit; they now seek to maximize their profits and, as such, are making more money now than ever before.

In fact, according to a recent report by Property Casualty Insurers Association of America, "Private U.S. property/casualty insurers' net income after taxes grew to $63.8 billion in 2013 from $35.1 billion in 2012 ...

Insurers' overall results for 2013 also benefited from a $4.6 billion increase in net investment gains—the sum of net investment income and realized capital gains (or losses) on investments—which rose to $58.8 billion in 2013 from $54.2 billion in 2012.

"'The $66.3 billion increase in policyholders' surplus to a record-high $653.3 billion at year-end 2013 is a testament to the strength and safety of insurers' commitment to policyholders. Insurers are strong, well-capitalized, and well prepared to pay future claims,' said Robert Gordon, PCI's senior vice president for policy development and research."[37]

Clearly, the property/casualty industry is alive and well in America, and it is not by accident. Insurance companies' ability to transfer the higher-risk loss events to government agencies and the changes instituted in claims handling since the recommendations of McKinsey and Accenture have led to a drastic increase in profitability. Whether it is the government, of which we are all taxpayers, or us as individuals, we are all bearing the increased cost of property insurance, and this trend is not likely to change for the better anytime soon.

Insurance companies, with their billions of dollars in profits, have significant influence over politicians, so it is unlikely that any substantial relief will come from government. And because many state insurance departments are filled with people who come from the insurance industry, it is safe to say that not all of these regulators are true consumer advocates. That being said, most of these agencies really try to protect the public from wrongful conduct, but internal budget restraints and the influence of the

---

[37] Property Casualty Insurers Association of America (http://www.pciaa.net/
     pciwebsite/Cms/Content/ViewPage?sitePageId=37458)

insurance industry often serve to work against the public's interests. As such, consumers can expect to continuously pay more and get less in the foreseeable future.

Notwithstanding the fact that the deck is significantly stacked against them, insurance consumers can still effectively get the coverage that they have paid for in the event of a loss, provided they enter the process with an understanding of just how the game is played. Winning in the game of claim negotiations takes training and skills that most claimants do not possess, but the ability to identify wrongful claim-settlement practices can help significantly in putting you on the road to a fair recovery.

Some of the most common improper claim practices have been examined in these pages, not to make the reader a claim adjuster, but to help consumers identify unfair treatment when they see it. Knowing that you are not being treated fairly by your adjuster is the first critical step to recovering the fair value of your claim. Whether you choose to do it yourself or you obtain assistance from an attorney or a public adjuster, an understanding of *The Claims Game* and how it is played can provide you a path to a full recovery of your loss and a little peace of mind.

APPENDIX I

Claim Basics 101

There is no way the lessons in this book can turn you into a claims adjuster and truly place you on equal footing with the insurance company; however, by following these simple steps, you may be able to prevent your claim from becoming the one that ends up in years of litigation. At the very least, heeding this advice will put you in a much better position for a fair claim settlement. If you are not willing to put in the effort to perform these simple steps, then you might seriously consider retaining professional representation.

The steps that we recommend below are the same steps that our professional adjusters follow and which all public adjusters should follow. Unfortunately, human beings have a tendency to be lazy, which often leads to good claims-handling practices being overlooked. We constantly are reminding our own adjusters of the importance of documenting the claim files to keep an accurate record of everything that happens on the claim, until the final check is received.

1. Do not sign a direct-pay authorization.

As mentioned in the previous chapter, the first step in a loss recovery is often to initiate emergency services to prevent further damages to the property. You will be told that protecting the property is your duty under the policy, and this is correct. Most often, the restoration contractor sent out by the insurance company, and even those who arrive at your door just after the loss happens, will present you with what they describe as simply a work-authorization form. But, most often, these forms contain a direct-payment authorization. This allows them to present their bills to the insurance company, and the insurance company is being told by your signature on their authorization that it is okay for them to pay the contractor directly.

Many consumers are never even told how much the emergency-services bills are before they are paid. This is a really bad idea. If you are unhappy with their work, or if they do other damages to your property, you have no recourse with them because they already have all of their money—your money. If they will not delete the direct-payment authorization from their contract, find another contractor who will. A reputable restoration contractor will not be afraid to stand behind their work.

2. Obtain a certified copy of the policy.

The first place to start in the processing of a claim is to know what is covered under the policy of insurance that was in place at the time of the loss. It is for this reason that our first request is for the production of a certified copy of the insurance policy. Doing this will insure that you are working from the correct policy for this loss. Policies change from year to year, so do not rely upon an old copy or even a new copy you may have in your insurance file. These policies may differ substantially from the policy in effect at the time of the current loss event.

Place your request to your insurer in writing, and keep a copy for your file. If they do not respond in a timely manner, contact your state department of insurance for assistance. Helping consumers get a copy of their insurance policy is one of the areas that these agencies really excel in, so don't be afraid to seek their assistance. The insurance company is required to provide you with this document upon request.

Read the policy to get a better understanding of the coverage provided and the terms of payment. This is not an easy task, which is why few people actually read their policies. If you are not willing to take the time to read your policy, you should seriously consider hiring professional representation. Unfortunately, even if you do read your policy, it is quite possible that you may not really understand it and the coverages it provides. This is because it is common for insurance policies to provide coverage in one section and then take it away or limit it in another section. In some of the more complex commercial policies, it is possible that the policy provides coverage, takes it away, and then gives it back, but limits it in another section. It can be difficult to understand exactly what the terms of your coverage are, but it is not impossible, with some effort.

3. Obtain a copy of the Unfair Claims Practices Act.

Go to the Internet and download a copy of your state's "Unfair Claims Practices" statutes. These can be found in your state insurance statutes, and they are easy to read and to understand. They give you, more or less, the playbook that the insurance company is required to follow. It provides information on the amount of time the adjuster has to investigate your claim, how long he has to respond to your written communications, and how long the company has to issue payment of your claim. Knowing these regulations can be very helpful in keeping your claim moving to conclusion.

4. Keep a claim log.

From day one, get a notebook and enter every activity that happens on your claim. Record every phone call, every meeting, and every claim activity, and make good notes as to exactly what was discussed and agreed upon. Even if you did not start a claim log on day one of your claim, start one right now, and go back in your mind and write down everything that you can remember. Your memory will not be any better two years from now when you are in court than it is today, so do not delay in doing this. And if your wife or husband or other relatives witnessed any of these meetings, have them write their own account of the meetings. Do not work together! Work separately because each person is likely to remember things the other did not, so by working separately and then combining these notes, you will have a better history of the claim.

While it may seem unlikely that your claim will ever go to litigation, if your claim process does proceed poorly, this log book will be an invaluable record of the claim events and will significantly help your case against the insurance company. As we tell our adjusters in our training seminars, "We always approach a new claim by hoping for the best but preparing for the worst."

We cannot tell you the numbers of times we hear new clients tell us that they made agreements with their adjuster and then their claim was reassigned to a new adjuster, who refuses to acknowledge or honor those agreements.

We recently had a client who reached an agreement with her adjuster for the repair of damages to her pool equipment caused by firefighting activities. She did not document this agreement before her claim was reassigned to another adjuster. The new adjuster refused to pay for these repairs, and when confronted with the fact that the other adjuster had agreed to these costs, he said that in his opinion, the damages were not caused by the fire department, and the previous adjuster had made no notes in this matter. Without any notation of the prior agreement, it was back to square one in getting the new adjuster's agreement to pay for these repairs. A simple e-mail to the prior adjuster confirming this agreement is all it would have taken to preserve the record of this agreement.

5.   Confirm all communications in writing.

It is critical that you document in writing every meeting and telephone call with the insurance company and with any of its contractors. These do not have to be full-blown legal letters, just a simple confirmation of a telephone call and what was discussed and agreed upon during the call, or confirmation of agreements made at a personal meeting. Ask the adjuster to provide a written explanation if you have misstated any of the agreements. Documenting the claims process is also important in preventing unreasonable delays in the processing of your claim. A simple letter confirming that the adjuster is working on his estimate and will have it done by Friday can be very effective in holding him accountable and moving your claim to a timely settlement.

When deciding what media to use, when dealing with insurance companies, a written letter is far more effective than an e-mail. Today, even though e-mail provides a written record of events, because it is so common in our everyday lives, people tend to view an e-mail just as though it were a telephone conversation. Hence, e-mails will work, but they are not as effective as written and mailed letters.

Also, many insurers have specific requirements of adjusters that require them to give a written response to letters received by the insurance company. From our experience, adjusters hate having to write letters, so a persistent written campaign can help push the timely settlement of your claim.

Be very careful what you put in a letter. Do not let your emotions get the best of you, and do not send something that might later be embarrassing to read in front of a jury. If you are too emotional, write it down and let it sit overnight before you send it, so that you have time to think about what you have said. Over the years, we have seen some shocking things said in writing by our clients to their adjuster and vice versa—like one who asked his adjuster if he beat his dog before or after his morning coffee. These comments, while they might feel good at the moment, are like winning a battle, when the objective is not to win a battle but to win the war.

Keeping an accurate record of each and every event throughout your claim process is of the utmost importance to getting a fair claim settlement. This written communication to the adjuster places him on notice that you are recording everything he or she does in regards to your claim. In our experience, a well-documented claim is one that usually gets paid faster and more fully.

6. Photograph everything.

As soon as possible, make a photographic record of all building damages and all personal property, damaged and undamaged. If possible, photograph personal-property items separately, even if there is only a trace of the damaged item, because insurance companies are constantly questioning the existence of property, even property they have already seen in their initial inspection. It is not uncommon for adjusters to get amnesia after they complete their initial loss inspection and the damaged property is already thrown away. Even after we reached an agreement with the adjuster on Bill and Ruth's claim in Chapter 1, six months later, the insurance adjuster was replaced by a new adjuster, and she continues to question the quantity of damaged items, even when provided with photographic evidence.

Also, thieves have a way of knowing when a property has had a loss, and they know the property is unlikely to be occupied. Even the theft of items that are a total loss can be problematic when trying to obtain payment for them from your insurance company. While the insurer still owes you for the items, it is much harder to prove that you had them and much more difficult to prove their value. Take tons of pictures! With today's digital media, it costs nothing to take a lot of pictures to save them as a record of your belongings.

We once had an insurance company questioning our client's claim submission, believing that they were claiming items that they did not have. As you can imagine, after a total-loss fire, there usually is very little evidence left. In this instance, the insurance company was questioning the existence of an exercise bike. We honestly could not remember the bike and were perplexed by how we were going to prove that our client had one. Then, when reviewing some of our photos taken the day of our first inspection of the building, there, in the rubble, was the frame and wheel from the exercise bike in question. We got lucky that this was in the picture, as it was not what we were taking a picture of, but submitting this photo to the insurer got our clients paid for the lost exercise bike.

While you are at it, get a video camera and take a good video of the property and all of the damaged contents. Video footage, coupled with photographs, can be very helpful in documenting your loss.

7. Do not throw away anything until you have the check in your hand.

Even if you have an agreement with the insurance company that certain items are a total loss and they have authorized you to throw them away, wait until you get your check; do not be suckered into thinking that you have a firm agreement with them. Hold onto all property until you have a written agreement from the insurer as to the value of these items, and then hold them until payment is received.

Just in case a new claim handler takes over your claim, you must protect yourself. What if you end up having to go to appraisal to determine the fair value of your loss? How will the appraisers know the true value of your items without being able to see them? Hold all property, regardless of its condition, until payment is received.

8. Do not start building repairs until you have a complete agreement in place.

Even though you may have a verbal agreement, we do not recommend starting repairs until you have the insurance company's position in writing and know for certain exactly what it is willing to pay you for your loss. If you alter the loss scene and later must demand appraisal to set the value of your loss, it can be much harder, in some instances, for the appraisers to really see your building as it was, and this can have a serious impact on the amount of your recovery.

What happens if you tear down a damaged wall and then the insurance company takes the position that that wall was not damaged by the loss, and they refuse to pay for it? How can you prove that the wall was damaged in the loss if it is already gone? We have had consumers bring hail-damage claims to us that are in dispute where they have already done a new coating over the damages. How can we prove it was damaged after the evidence has been destroyed?

Do not start any work until a complete settlement agreement has been reached. It is not in your best interest to change the loss scene until then. Insurers often pressure customers to start demolition before the claim settlement has been finalized. They sometimes suggest that it is your duty under the policy to mitigate your loss. While it is true that you, as the policyholder, do have a duty to mitigate your loss, this does not mean that you must start repairs before you know how much money you will have to complete the restoration. If your adjuster tells you this, tell him that you cannot contract for the repairs until you know how much money the insurance company is going to pay you to complete the repairs. Starting the work before you have a final agreement only benefits the insurance company.

We have had clients that ignored our warnings and moved forward with repairs, only to find out that the insurance company was not in agreement with the scope of repairs to their building. How can you prove that replacing your roof was the only logical means to restoring your roof, rather than just some partial repair, once the roof has been replaced?

Also, who will end up making up the difference, if your contractor starts making repairs that the insurance company eventually refuses to pay for?

That's right—it may come out of your pocket. As much as you may be in a hurry to get your property repaired as quickly as possible, you must be patient until you have the insurance company's written agreement and their check.

9. Obtain the full policy benefits for replacement of buildings and personal property.

Insurance policies differ somewhat on the replacement-cost benefits offered and what is required to obtain them, but under most standard-form replacement-cost insurance policies, the insurance company does not have to pay you the full replacement-cost value of your claim until you actually make the repairs or replacements.

Before getting into the details on how these policy requirements work, let us start by explaining some of the terminology that is used in insurance. The term *replacement cost value,* or RCV, means just that; it is the current replacement cost of the item that is being replaced. The term *actual cash value,* or ACV, is, in most jurisdictions, the replacement-cost value of the item minus an amount called depreciation to account for the age or wear and tear of the item. What is left is the actual cash value of that item. Most policies written today only require the insurance company to pay you the actual cash value of your loss until repairs are completed.

Therefore, it is critical that you do not assume that simply completing repairs or replacements will result in another check for the full amount of the depreciation the insurer is holding, which is usually referred to as a *depreciation holdback.* Insurance companies word these policies for their own benefit, not for yours. If they can sell you the illusion of replacement-cost coverage and never have to pay up fully, then they win. Do you remember McKinsey's reference to insurance being a zero-sum game?

There are ways to recover your full replacement-cost value, if you know how to play their game and if you are very diligent in tracking the replacement of items. The following examples will help to understand how these loss-payment provisions work and enable you to more fully recover the replacement value of your loss.

Personal Property Example

Let's assume that you lost a fifty-five-inch TV in a fire. The insurance company has agreed that the replacement cost of this TV is $800, but because it was four years old, they have taken off 40 percent, or $320, from your claim payment for depreciation, leaving you with $480 to buy a new TV. So you go down to Walmart and find that they have fifty-five-inch TVs on sale for $675. You are thrilled by your luck in finding this item on sale, so you buy it, expecting to submit the receipt and get your $320 check.

Not so fast; most of these policies are worded in a manner so that you get the $800 only if you actually spend $800. If you spend less, the insurance company's obligation is for the lesser of either the replacement-cost value or the actual amount spent. So instead of getting a check for $320, you get a check for $195.

Congratulations! By buying this item on sale, you just saved the insurance company $125. If you understand how this works up front, you are enabled to make better buying decisions. Maybe now, understanding how this replacement-cost system works, you might decide to buy a slightly better or different model. Most insurance companies do not care which model of TV you buy as a replacement. They only care that you purchase a similar TV and that you spent the full agreed-upon replacement cost on it.

Assume that your damaged television was a Sony fifty-five-inch set. Let's assume that Best Buy does not have a Sony fifty-five-inch inch set but has a Sony sixty-inch TV on sale for $850. If you decide to go this route, you will need to kick in the fifty-dollar difference yourself, but in the end, you will have maximized the benefits of your policy, and for a small additional investment, you have a much nicer replacement TV. If you are happy with the cheaper replacement TV, that is your choice, but at least it is a conscious decision.

We suggest that you go through the entire list of total-loss property and highlight those items that you need to replace first and those items with the largest depreciation-holdback values. Make a plan for replacing these items in your first wave of replacements while you have the ACV insurance check in hand.

Do not give the insurer your original receipts; provide them with copies of these receipts. If they insist on obtaining the original receipts, offer, in writing, for them to come over to your home and let them look at any receipt they like and allow them to make copies, but we recommend that you not allow them to take possession of them, as all too often, policyholders never get them back. You may need these receipts for warranty claims if the product fails within the store's replacement policy or for proof of purchase for in-warranty repairs.

We are often asked by our clients if they can substitute one item for another. For instance, let's say you had a sofa and loveseat in your home, but you want to replace them with a sofa and a recliner chair. This substitution would qualify for recovery of the depreciation-holdback money that was set aside by your insurer, because this replacement, while not exactly the same items, serves the same function that the lost items served. The same types of substitutions can be made with the replacement of movies on VHS tapes with movies on Blu-ray discs. The policy requires that you replace items with ones for similar use, so as long as you do not stray too far from the original property, the insurer should honor the replacement and issue payment.

The insurer is holding your money, and most policies have time limits on making claims for these depreciation-holdback benefits. Be certain to get a full and complete copy of your policy, and have the adjuster highlight the areas that affect your recovery of the policy benefits. Pay close attention to time limits on submitting requests for depreciation-holdback monies.

But do not give up on recovering the holdback money if there are extenuating circumstances that prevented you from completing the replacements within the policy's allotted time period. Many states have laws that prevent insurance companies from strictly applying the policy's "forfeiture" language when their own acts have prevented the timely replacement of property. In other words, if you have one year to submit your receipts for replacement, but the insurance company takes nine months to settle your claim, many courts will "toll" the period for replacement by the amount of time consumed in the settlement process. Check with an attorney for the laws on this issue in your jurisdiction.

The insurance company will be looking for any excuse to not pay this holdback money to you, and even when it does pay, do not expect a check immediately. We often see clients waiting for weeks and even months to get their depreciation-holdback money. Remember, the entire insurance system is designed to delay their claim payments and to discourage you from making claims for all of your benefits. The harder they make the process, the better it is for them because it is a fact that many people will just give up rather than be persistent. And by requiring policyholders to jump through all of these hoops to get the full policy benefits, they know many people will not play this game and will settle for just the actual cash value payment.

Building Property Example

In this example, let's assume that you have settled your insurance claim for fire damage to your commercial building for $250,000 at replacement-cost value and with a $165,000 actual cash value. The insurer is holding $85,000 of your money and is looking at any excuse to not pay this money to you. It is human nature to try to get the best deal on something. No one wants to pay the highest price for an item; we all want to buy it "below wholesale."

So you make a deal to have your brother-in-law, who works in construction, make the repairs on your building. The same requirements for collecting your depreciation holdback on your personal property applies to getting the depreciation-holdback payment on the building damages. You must prove that you spent the full replacement-cost value to obtain the full amount of depreciation holdback.

An insurance policy is not designed to put money in your pocket; it is designed to indemnify you for your actual loss. So in your quest to get the best price from your contractor or to save money on the construction, you must keep in mind that paying less may mean getting less indemnity from your insurance company. Most insurers do not care as much about how you spend the money as they do about the fact that you spent it and made the repairs they paid for. This can give you some flexibility as you negotiate with contractors for your restoration project.

If you can get the contractor to throw in a few extras or upgrades to flooring or cabinets to get your contract, all the better for you, and this is the area that can provide you the best value for your money. But be very careful when contracting for these repairs. Be sure that the contract specifies the full replacement-cost value that has been agreed upon with the insurance company. And be certain that the final payment to the contractor is predicated upon your receipt of this indemnity from the insurance company. Insurance companies can be extremely slow in their payment of depreciation-holdback monies, often taking weeks or even months to remit a check. Do not place yourself in a default situation with your contractor on the final payment under the contract. Be certain that you and the contractor are both on the same page on payments under his restoration contract.

10. Use the policy's benefits to obtain suitable and equivalent temporary housing.

Many insurers and their agents try to limit their liability for additional living-expense benefits by either not informing consumers of their rights to this coverage at all or by encouraging them to move into a substantially smaller temporary home or maybe an apartment. They often reason that it is only temporary, and most consumers are also under the impression that their relocation will only be temporary and are willing to tolerate a smaller residence for a short period of time.

But what happens when your stay becomes much longer than expected? Agreeing to move into a house or apartment that is far smaller and has less amenities than your damaged home had only saves the insurance company money. We often hear our consumers tell us that they accepted a much cheaper temporary home because they wanted to be fair to the insurance company and save it money. They are usually surprised when their efforts to be courteous to the insurer are not reciprocated by a full and fair settlement of their claim.

Moving into a home that does not have the swimming pool your home has or the extra bedrooms for guests that yours has does not win you any favor with insurance companies. All it does is make you less comfortable in these temporary circumstances than you would be if you rented a comparable property to your own. And there is another possibly unforeseen benefit to insisting upon comparable temporary housing: the cost of providing these benefits to the insurance company.

Let's assume that after weeks of negotiations, you reach an impasse with your insurer on the cost of repairing your home. The monthly cost of your temporary housing can be an advantage to getting this difference settled. Assume that the difference between your and the insurance company's estimates on your home's damages is $30,000 and your temporary housing costs are $7,000 per month. If you were to demand appraisal, the time it will take to complete the appraisal process—usually at least three months, and possibly more—will cost the insurance company an additional $21,000, plus whatever additional amounts you recover in the appraisal process. This places you on more equal ground to negotiate a reasonable compromise resolution of your claim.

Hence, the benefits of insisting upon comparable temporary housing are that you are more comfortable, should you need to stay longer than expected, and it gives the insurance company a greater incentive to settle your loss and get you back into your home quickly.

Also, do not let yourself be suckered into taking less in the form of amenities, either. If your home had three televisions, the insurance company owes you for three rental televisions in the temporary home. If your home has a garage, you are entitled to a temporary home with a garage. If you have a swimming pool, they owe you for a temporary home with a pool. If the only available homes have amenities that your home did not have, then they owe you one of these homes as temporary housing.

They also must rent furnishings and a complete housewares package that includes pots, pans, towels, dishes, etc. The policy owes for the increased cost of maintaining your "normal standard of living," which is generally viewed as a home of similar size and amenities and as close as possible to your home neighborhood. They cannot make you drive all the way across town to save them money on your temporary-housing claim.

There are so many pitfalls to avoid in the handling of a large-loss property claim that it is simply impossible to cover everything here. However, if you follow the above steps, you will have at least set the stage for a successful outcome of your claim. Be diligent in your record-keeping and documentation, so that hopefully, you will never need it. And most importantly, confirm everything in writing to your adjuster; it is amazing what short memories they can have. If it is in writing, you have a record of events that you can use to get what was promised.

APPENDIX II

Choosing a Public Adjuster

Experiencing catastrophic damage to your home or business can be highly disruptive and traumatic. The decisions you make early in the claim process can have a profound effect on not only your ultimate recovery but also on your mental well-being. Choosing the right public adjuster to represent you in the settlement of your insurance claim is a very important decision. Choosing the right adjuster will provide clarity to the process, enable you to focus on your business or family, and significantly impact your recovery from the loss. Choosing the wrong public adjuster can make an already dreadful situation a nightmare.

Not all public adjusters are created equal. Public adjusters are no different than people in any other profession; there are both good and bad practitioners. Regrettably, when it comes to public adjusters, there are probably more bad ones than good ones. The reason for this is because there is no real school to train public adjusters. Many sole-proprietor public adjusters start their careers working for insurance companies and learn how to handle claims from them.

Unfortunately, the business of representing the consumer is very different from representing the interests of an insurance company. For one thing, insurance companies have claims managers overseeing the adjuster's work and scores of attorneys to provide guidance when a difficult coverage or legal questions arise. Also, very few public adjusters have the opportunity to learn the consumer side of adjusting under the guidance of a competent mentor. Add to this the fact that nearly anyone with reasonable intelligence can pass the state public-adjuster licensing exams with just a few days of study and you have created a system that is designed to produce many poorly trained and/or unqualified public adjusters.

Many states have enacted continuing-education requirements, which is a step in the right direction, but these requirements come after these new adjusters are already licensed. Until they actually know what they are doing, do you really want them handling your claim? You have heard the saying, "Knowledge is power." When it comes to the business of public adjusting, this phrase could not be more insightful.

The fact is, some public adjusters are better qualified than others. Some demonstrate higher levels of professional integrity. Some have more experience in handling certain types of claims. The key is to find the right adjuster with the right qualifications for your loss situation. Finding the right public adjuster requires a little of your time, but the cost of not properly vetting your chosen public adjuster can be so astronomical that the time invested is a small price to pay for the peace of mind of knowing that you have a true professional protecting your interests.

So how do you go about finding a professional instead of a pretender? To start with, do not rush into a decision on representation, and, especially, do not hire the first public adjuster that shows up at your door after a loss. While he may ultimately prove to be the best qualified and the best choice for representation, you cannot possibly know that yet. You need to take some time to research his credentials and references. Requesting and researching the following information will help you to choose the right public adjuster.

- Request his professional resume. After all, he is applying for a job, to be your claim representative, so it is completely reasonable to request his curriculum vitae. If he cannot produce one or is apprehensive to do so, do not hire him.
- Verify his formal and insurance-specific education. Confirm his claims-handling experience. This information should be on his

resume and is easily verified by asking for a diploma or contacting the educator's referenced.

- Meet personally with the adjuster who will be assigned to handle your claim. Some of the bigger firms send out charming solicitors to secure business, but you could end up with an adjuster that you do not care for. Do not hire a company without first meeting the adjuster assigned to handle your claim.
- Confirm that he will handle your claim in accordance with the steps that have been outlined in Appendix I. Handling claims in this manner takes a great deal more time, which is why many adjusters take shortcuts in their claims handling, But following these steps is the only way to professionally handle an insurance claim.
- Documentation is critical. Get a commitment that he will create a written record of every claim event.
- Develop a list of questions you might have about your claim, and ask how he intends to handle your claim. Also, ask him about other similar claims he has handled.
- Verify his business address and telephone number. Some public adjusters work out of the trunks of their cars and receive their mail at a mailbox store. If your claim develops problems, it may be difficult to find this guy when you need him most. It is generally better to work with a legitimate firm that has a real office and a staff to assist you when your adjuster is busy on another claim or otherwise out of touch. We constantly hear complaints from the customers of other public adjusters who say that their public adjuster does not return their calls and has not been in touch with them for weeks. These types of problems can be eliminated by hiring a public adjuster who has a business that is structured to serve the public.
- Ask for his list of current references, and call them. Ask them questions about how this public adjuster handled their claim and how attentive he was in communicating to them throughout the claim process. Be aware that most public adjusters will load their references with their best customers, so ask for a couple references to clients whose claims did not go smoothly.

- Check with the Department of Insurance to verify that his license and his firm's license are active and in good standing.
- Ask him to produce evidence of errors and omissions insurance coverage. This protects you if he makes a major mistake in the handling of your claim that causes a forfeiture of policy benefits. If he does not have this insurance, do not hire him.
- Ask him to produce evidence of workmen's compensation insurance. This protects you if he falls off your roof or is otherwise injured on your property. If he does not have this, do not hire him.
- Ask him to produce evidence of business-liability insurance. This insurance can provide you other protections, should a situation arise from his claim-handling activities. If he does not have this insurance, do not hire him.
- Check consumer organizations such as the Better Business Bureau (BBB) for their records on the firm and their complaint history. Keep in mind that even the best public adjuster will occasionally have an unhappy client if he or she has been in business for any length of time. If the complaint is closed satisfactorily, then it is probably not a big deal. However, if he has a history of multiple unresolved complaints, this should be a warning sign to stay away.
- Interview more than one public adjuster. You will find that their qualifications may vary, and there is the personal element to representation, as this is someone you must work closely with over the next few months. Find someone you get along with and who is attentive to your needs. Of course, remember, this is not a popularity contest, so keep that in mind too, but personalities make a difference when working closely with someone.
- Discuss the fees that will be charged. Keep in mind that the lowest fee does not always result in more money in your pocket. A highly qualified professional may charge a higher fee, but if he greatly increases the total recovery, this could result in a much better bargain than the guy with the cheapest fee who does little to increase the claim settlement value.

Beware of the solicitors who attempt to sell you their services by telling you they will beat everyone's lowest fee to get your business. These types of public adjusters generally do not add value to your claim but rely upon taking their fees off the top of the insurance company's settlement offer and do little work to increase your recovery.

- Look at the adjuster's professional affiliations. Memberships in nationally recognized or regional adjusting groups show that he is probably serious about continuing education and professionalism. Look for membership in organizations like NAPIA (National Public Insurance Adjuster Association), TAPIA (Texas Public Insurance Adjuster Association), RMAPIA (Rocky Mountain Association of Public Insurance Adjusters), or FAPIA (Florida Association of Public Insurance Adjusters).

Even more importantly, look for individuals that maintain membership in professional insurance-education associations, as these are the adjusters who are truly committed to professional insurance education—groups like the SCLA (Society of Claims Law Associates), CPCU (Chartered Property Casualty Underwriters Society), and the CLM (Claims and Litigation Management Alliance). These organizations offer professional designations for completion of insurance-education programs and hold in-depth continuing-education programs. Regrettably, very few public adjusters engage in this type of intensive continuing-insurance education.

Timing of Hiring a Public Adjuster

When is the best time to retain a public adjuster? This depends upon the size and complexity of your claim and, to a lesser degree, the luck of the draw with respect to the adjuster assigned to your claim. We are occasionally and pleasantly surprised to find a competent professional company adjuster on the other side of a claim. Regrettably, this is by far the exception rather than the rule in today's claims environment. That being said, there is occasionally a claim situation that does not require professional representation.

We recently had a claim like this in Texas, where the loss was well in excess of the policy's coverage, so after our review of the claim, we explained that there was no need for our services. Similarly, we recently had a claim in Illinois on a total fire loss to a grocery store. On this claim, just a few days after we were hired, the adjuster agreed to pay the policy limits for the structure, so we voluntarily agreed to modify our contract and took only a percentage of any new recoveries we achieved. [38] In this case, we were able to use several of the additional-coverages provisions of the policy to increase his settlement by an additional $42,000, plus a sizable recovery for his loss of business income.

You should not be in a rush to hire anyone, but our experience shows that having your claim representative in place early in the claim process is preferable for a large or complex loss. An experienced adjuster can help you to make decisions that are the most beneficial to you and that may not be the decisions that the company's adjuster will suggest. A public adjuster is not concerned with the insurance company's profits, but with helping you to get into a more stable and suitable situation so that you can focus on your family or your business during the recovery process.

A public adjuster can present you options that often are not communicated by the insurance company's adjuster; options like using the policy's extra-expense coverage to establish a temporary business location or purchasing products from a competitor to fill your customers' current orders so that you don't lose their business permanently.

We recently handled a tortilla manufacturing business claim where we arranged to purchase tortillas from a competitor until their operation could be restored. This action saved them from permanently losing their customers.

---

[38] Some states have regulations that prevent the charging of fees in these situations. In this case, the law was silent, but integrity wasn't.

On an auto shop claim in California, the owner had two garage buildings with several auto repair bays in each, all on the same electrical system. He had always wanted to separate the electric to make each building independent of the other so that he could rent the smaller of these buildings. When a fire destroyed the larger building, we were able to use the policy's extra-expense coverage to install a separate electric meter to the undamaged building to be used as a temporary shop. He ultimately benefited from this electrical work and it did not affect his building recovery which ended up exceeding his policy limits.

A good public adjuster can often use these policy provisions to protect the business's financial future from losses long after it is restored. Insurance companies don't really care what happens to the business after it is restored, and they are off the hook for payments under the policy, so they may not advise or encourage these types of extra-expense expenditures.

We are often contacted weeks and months after a loss, when a claim has become a huge problem, to assist in correcting the situation. It is important to recognize that some prior actions or decisions cannot be undone and they can significantly impact your claim recovery. It is a fine line between being too quick to hire representation and too late. We cannot help you know where this line is drawn, as each claim is as unique as a fingerprint.

APPENDIX III

Choosing an Attorney

As with those of public adjusters, attorneys' qualifications can vary drastically. While an attorney with a law license can legally represent you in a claim situation, not every attorney is intimately familiar with insurance-claims handling, and few have the litigation experience necessary to take on and defeat the insurance companies' legions of defense attorneys. It is rare indeed to have an experienced bad-faith attorney willing to engage in the processing of a claim.

Just as you would not go to a podiatrist for brain surgery, hiring an attorney who does not routinely work in insurance bad-faith litigation is a recipe for disaster. Some of the worst situations we have experienced with our clients were the result of their retention of an attorney who was unfamiliar with insurance bad-faith litigation. Not long ago, we had a client who hired his old college buddy who had gone on to law school after college. His friend was going to help him out with his claim situation and sue the insurance company for bad faith, but in the end, he got very poor results, and it was clear to us that he did not know how to create value to get a good settlement. This is not how you want to choose your legal counsel.

The quickest way to find attorneys familiar with insurance bad faith is to ask several public adjusters for referrals. Most public adjusters work routinely with bad-faith attorneys and are more than happy to provide a reference. Get recommendations from several public adjusters because most have one or two attorneys whom they favor, possibly for reasons other than their legal abilities. We generally recommend finding two or three attorneys when it is time to litigate a claim matter because personalities matter when you are going down the two- to three-year road of litigation. Finding someone who is the right fit is important.

Like some public adjusters, many insurance bad-faith attorneys are lazy. They want to push for a quick claim settlement that requires them to do the least amount of work. Some of our biggest frustrations are with attorneys our clients have chosen, without our input and three months into the litigation process, when they call up and tell us that they have settled the case in mediation. We know that three months is not enough time to have completed any reasonable discovery, so essentially, they have sold the claim out for a quick, easy fee and have convinced the consumer that this is really the best deal for him or her. We have had some very good litigations destroyed like this, and it is extremely frustrating when we put so much hard work into thoroughly documenting the insurance company's wrongful actions and behavior, only to achieve nickels on the dollar in the claim resolution.

To protect yourself, do your research. Find an attorney with a reputation for aggressiveness and with a history of large insurance recoveries. Find an attorney who has engaged in a reasonable number of insurance bad-faith trials. Many attorneys who practice in insurance bad faith have not seen the inside of a courtroom in years. We have met attorneys who we believe were intimidated by the idea of trying a case. Find an attorney who does insurance bad-faith litigation as the focus of his or her practice. These attorneys have developed intimate knowledge of insurance-company processes and know how to create value for your case through targeted discovery requests and through tactfully filing motions to compel discovery and to limit their defenses.

To put it another way, they know "where the bodies are buried," so they know how to get to the insurance company's Achilles heel. Remember that insurance companies are experts in evaluating risk. When your attorney has created enough risk for them, they will be more motivated to settle with you closer to your terms than theirs. It takes a tremendous amount of work and knowledge of the insurance-litigation process to get to this point, but many of our clients that have survived this process, will tell you that it was worth it.

AUTHOR'S NOTE

The conduct described in this book is not an indictment of every insurance company or of every adjuster or of the processing of all claims. While the problems with claims handling are becoming epidemic, there are still a handful of good and ethical company and independent adjusters working to fulfill the insurer's promise of coverage.

Unfortunately, these folks are becoming fewer and farther between, as they reach retirement and are replaced with ambitious young adjusters who have been indoctrinated into the insurance companies' new profit-focused mindset. We know of many of these "old pros," who are biding their time until they reach retirement age. Many have spoken privately to us on the changes the claims industry has seen over the last ten years, and most are glad to be getting out. Others simply roll their eyes to us at site inspections, more or less admitting their understanding of the inappropriateness of the claim position they are being forced to pursue, while acknowledging their inability to do anything about it.

With this in mind, we want to pay tribute here to those true claims professionals with whom we deal with on a daily basis. We know who you are, and we respect you.